WEAVING YOU CAN DO

WEAVING
You Can Do

By EDITH LOUISE ALLEN

The MANUAL ARTS PRESS, *Peoria, Illinois*

CONTENTS

Chapter V

PATTERN PROBLEMS

Right and Wrong Sides of Fabrics • Names of Threading Patterns • Producing Different Effects on One Threading • Limitations in Pattern Weaving • Weavers Often Specialize • How Textures May Be Developed in Fabrics • Narrow Fabrics Woven Side by Side • Buttonholes • Fringe • Leno or Lace Weaves • Double-Surface Weaving • Double Weaving • Bead Weaving • Card Weaving • Weaving on an Inkle Loom • Variety of Weaves in This Chapter

INDEX

CHAPTER I

Getting the Right Start
Toward Beautiful Weaving

Tʜɪs book gives the basic weaves from which an unlimited variety of materials may be made; an understanding of looms; and how one person alone can proceed in the art of weaving. Methods requiring the aid of helpers have been omitted.

It will help those with a longing to weave, whether they can assemble only a few sticks of wood to form a loom or can afford any equipment they desire.

Work Space

Space for storage and use of weaving appliances is often a problem; therefore it may be comforting to know that small or folding looms are available as well as the large, massive ones. No one needs to be discouraged, for many of the most beautiful fabrics have been woven with very little equipment. In fact, it is advisable to begin with simple devices.

Value of Simple Methods

The methods and designs discussed here are those which are useful in all types of weaving, and which leave nothing to be unlearned when one does more advanced work.

Designers of fabrics often use small looms because they can plan and experiment while they are weaving. Hand weaving on a small scale has its own value, as hand-woven material is the craftsman's individual creation, therefore interesting to him. Another value is that the practice of weaving well done fastens habits of painstaking workmanship on the weaver and develops his taste and love for things excellently and thoughtfully fabricated. The amateur is advised to be satisfied only with the highest standard of work, for it is the attainment of high standards which makes his product worth while. Simple forms of weaving should be attempted first in order to know exactly what makes good work and to understand what is taking place when more complicated devices and patterns are used.

Coverage in This Book

Weaving is the crossing and interlacing of threads or fibers to form cloth. Weaving taken up in this book is the type that is done on some sort of frame which forms the basis of a loom. The types known as *plaiting* or *braiding*, and *looping*, which includes *knitting* and *crocheting*, *netting*, *tatting*, *coiling*, and *twining*, are not discussed.

Definition of a Loom

A loom is a frame or machine used to hold one set of threads, called warp, in order while other threads, called weft, woof, or filler, are interlaced with the warp. See Fig. 1. The more elaborate, machinelike looms merely assist in the interweaving of the threads.

Warp and Weft

Warp threads run lengthwise of the loom on which they are stretched and form the skeleton of the fabric. The weft is put in at right angles and binds them together, thus completing the cloth. An exception is found when using a frame made for darning weaves, as on such looms the warp and the weft may run in more than one direction.

Fig. 1. Artist's canvas stretcher used for a loom. Note angle irons reinforcing the corners. Nos. 1 and 8 are boards nailed to the frame to raise the warp. Nos. 2, 3, and 7 are sticks used to space the warp. Nos. 2 and 3 make a cross to keep it in order. No. 3 happens to be a homemade shuttle which in this position can be used to make a shed. No. 9 — another home-made shuttle. No. 4 — a dowel rod or leash stick with leash string attached. No. 6 — coarse material used to start the weaving. No. 5 — Some weaving of the weft-face type. The warp is wound around the loom. Some weft is on the shuttle.

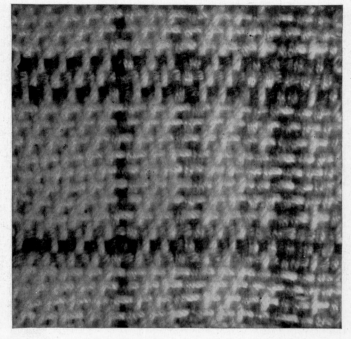

Fig. 2. Piece of tabby weave made on a frame loom.

Basis of Designs

All designs result from the infinite number of ways in which warp and weft may be crossed, and the different effects produced by the great variety of fibers, sizes, textures, and colors in the threads used.

Darning

Darning is a simple form of weaving. When carefully done the result is a bit of plain- or tabby-woven cloth which fills a hole. In darning, there are warp threads which are the first stretched across the portion of material to be mended. As they are put in, it is necessary to stretch the work on the hand, or in

10

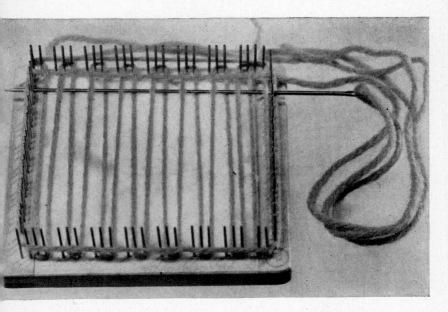

Fig. 3. Weaving frame for making squares of cloth with selvages on all four sides. Yarn around outside makes little larger square than in Fig. 5. A long needle is used for a shuttle.

an embroidery hoop, or with a "mending egg" to enable one to darn evenly. Any one of these represents the loom in its simplest form. With a needle, which represents a shuttle, a thread (which is the weft) is worked under and over the warp to form the fabric. Plain or tabby weaving thus formed is the same in construction as that made on any loom. Incidentally, this is the most used of all weaves and often forms the foundation for more intricate patterns. See Figs. 2 and 3.

CHAPTER II

Weaves Made on a Weaving Frame

Squares and oblongs may be woven in darning weaves on a small frame with grooved edges or small-head finishing nails over which the warp is wound. Having these grooves or nails in rows on all sides insures four straight edges. The yarn is first wound through the grooves or around the nails lengthwise, usually beginning at the near left-hand corner. See Figs. 3 and 4. It is sometimes wound crosswise or may be wound diagonally. The winding depends on the pattern and the thickness of the cloth to be made. The tension of the yarn should be even and rather loose. After the warp is on the loom, a thread long enough to weave from side to side of the frame from top to bottom, and a little more, is measured by wrapping the yarn around the rim of the loom. Each time around is equal to four cross weft on a square frame. The number of times it is put around depends on the pattern to be woven. Eight is a common number. After being measured, it is threaded into the long needle which reaches across the loom; this needle is worked over and under the warp as in darning. It may be threaded again and worked across at right angles or later diagonally to the first weaving. Variations are also made by skipping over some warp in regular order. The finished pieces are often sewed or crocheted together to make larger articles. Note from the diagram, Fig. 5, how the winding is done to make the threads run straight across the loom.

Fig. 4. A square of cloth made on a frame like the one in Fig. 3.

Yarn Needed for Purse, Mat, and Bag

To make a zipper purse 5½ x 6½ inches, 12½ yards of tapestry wool of one color and 64 of another are required.

A plate mat requires 90 yards of background yarn and 10 yards of another color.

A knitting bag, 8 x 11 inches, requires 4 skeins of 36 yards each and three skeins of 12 yards each of other colors. See Fig. 6.

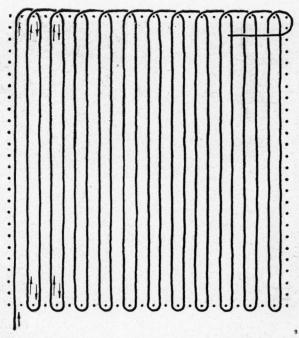

Fig. 5. Diagram of a way to put yarn on a weaving frame. This winding makes the warp go straight across the frame.

Weaving on Board and Frame Looms

Many types of weaving may be duplicated **on board and frame looms.** See Figs. 1 and 7. If one cannot attend a school, the easiest and soundest way to learn weaving is to begin on the previously described loom. Then try each of the various steps and methods of handling the warp and weft in making different materials. By doing this one learns what each gadget on the more mechanized loom is for and how it operates. Furthermore, one learns what type of weaving one likes best and how much of an investment is desirable for equipment.

The loom illustrated in Fig. 7 consists of a board about 12 inches

14

Fig. 6. A block of wood used for a loom. A handbag is being woven on it with a needle.

wide and 26 inches long, with a piece of wood fastened to each end to raise the warp up from the board. The one in Fig. 1 is made of four pieces of wood fastened securely together at the four corners so that the frame will be rigid. Pieces of wood may also be attached to raise the warp above the sides of the frame.

Small useful articles for home or gifts, such as pot holders, towels, place mats, and handbag covers, may result from trial weaving. While making such articles, the beginner should experiment by varying the spacing, color, number, size, and texture of the warp and weft used. See Fig. 8.

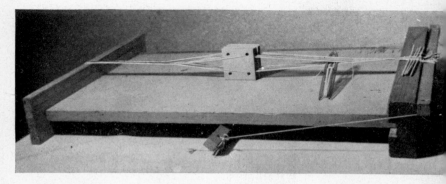

Fig. 7. Board loom with card weaving started on it. The wood attached to the ends raises the warp above the board so the weft may be passed through easily. Weaving with cards is discussed later.

Warping a Frame or Board Loom

The simplest and quickest way to put warp on one of these looms is to wind it around and around lengthwise. See Fig. 1. When this is done, one or more small pieces of weaving may be made on each side. Candle wicking, cotton rug yarn, strips of cloth, or heavy cord make good material for experimental purposes, and pot holders are a good article to begin with, as they are small and quickly finished. However, the weaver should be satisfied only when each pot holder is perfectly woven. Taking out mistakes is not difficult when making such articles.

For making pot holders from cotton rug yarn, wind on 75 warp threads. Count to see that this number of strands is on each side — that is, back and front. The beginning and final ends of the warp can be secured to small screw eyes or nails which may be removed when no longer wanted, or they may be tied to the frame. When the warp is on, a thin stick, like an extra-long pencil, should be put over and under the alternating strands of warp and pushed down to one end of the frame. A second stick is put under the lower threads and over the upper ones, then

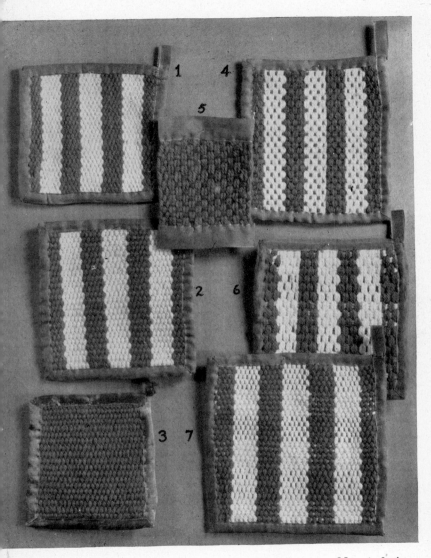

Fig. 8. Pot holders. The warp for the five two-color ones, Nos. 1, 2, 4, 6, and 7, was put on the loom, and they were woven one after another. The differences in them is due to the closeness with which the warp was pushed together and the manner of putting the weft over and under the warp. The weave affected the size of the holders. The plain tabby weave, No. 7, made the largest one. The basket weave made the smallest one.

pushed against the first stick to help prevent the warp from getting crossed in the process of weaving. This is sometimes called "making a cross in the warp." See Fig. 1, Nos. 2 and 3. Next make bobbinlike balls from the yarn to be used for weft. See Fig. 13, page 22.

Plain or Tabby Weaving (Figs. 8, 9, and 39)

Hold the frame with the cross made by the sticks away from the body, and lift the alternating warp threads with the fingers while putting the little bobbin of yarn under them in succession, taking care that none are missed or pushed out of order. This puts the weft from the bobbin in place. It should be pushed toward the weaver with the fingers, or better still, with the nearest stick in the warp, or with a comb. After one "shot" or "pick" of weft is in place at right angles to the warp, put in another by lifting the threads not lifted before. Press this down close to the first and repeat. The comb in this case represents the reed or beater of a table or floor loom. When two or more picks of weft or filler have been put in, it will be noted that half the warp which is over the nearest stick may be raised all at one time by lifting the stick enough to let the little ball pass under all the warp above it.

A Shed Stick (Fig. 1, No. 3)

A flat stick like a ruler is better than a round one for lifting warp, as it may be quickly turned on edge to make room for the ball to pass. The space made by turning the stick on edge is called a shed. This is an improvement over lifting half the warp with the fingers.

Finger Weaves: Indian Tie, Sumak, Single Warp, and Tapestry

Indian Tie. After the warp is put on and spaced eight or less to an inch, depending on the size of the weft, an inch of plain

18

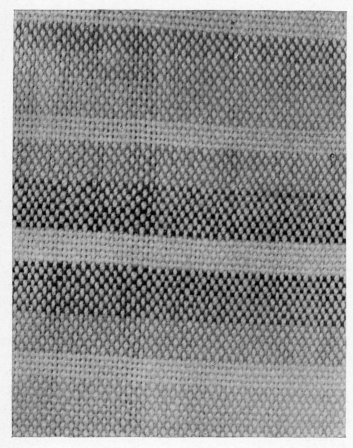

Fig. 9. Plain or tabby weave made on a floor loom. *Woven in Loom Craft Studio, Wilmington, Ohio.*

over-and-under or tabby is made for a hem. The loom is now ready for a type of finger weaving commonly used by Indians and called Indian tie. See Fig. 10. The ends of two balls of yarn are tied together. Starting with the knot at the outside of the first warp thread at either the right or left, have one ball

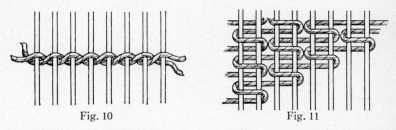

Fig. 10   Fig. 11

Fig. 10. Diagram of Indian tie weave. Fig. 11. Diagram showing how to put in the filler in sumak weave. As each row of filler is put in, it is pressed down firmly against the last pick of binding weft. The binding weft is not shown in the diagram.

below and one above the warp. Then pass them between the first two warp. Pass them back between the next two. This makes a cross of yarn between each pair of warp. As rows of weft are put in, they are pressed down close to the preceding ones so that the warp is entirely covered. Designs are made by having balls of different colors, or pairs for each color needed. Short lengths of yarn may be folded at the center for weft. When the color is to be changed, the one being used is turned back over the last warp reached. The new color is started by being placed around the same warp. When the weaving is well under way, the beginning of new weft need not be knotted for the ends may be pressed in between the other rows.

Sumak. Sumak is a finger weave used in making rugs, table covers, upholstery, and other heavy materials. See Fig. 11. A filler is put in without making a shed and a finer tabby weft is alternated with it for binding, and to keep the material from stretching. Being larger and softer than the warp and the binding, the filler entirely covers them. The warp is spaced eight to fourteen to an inch and should be of strong linen or cotton. An edge of tabby made from the binding weft provides material for a hem or adding fringe. It also makes an even beginning for the material. The filler is put in by passing it under four warp

20

and then back over two and again under four, which is repeated back and forth across the warp. The end of filler extending beyond the warp at the beginning is laid over the first few uncovered warp and secured in place when the filler is returned to this side of the loom. This step may be omitted when

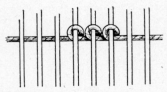

making seat covers, as the edges will not show and it is desirable to have them slightly thinner than the center. To return the filler across the web, carry it entirely around the two warp at the beginning of the next row back under 4 and over 2, as for the first weaving. As soon as one or two rows of filler are in place, a shot or pick or two of binding in tabby goes next, then more filler. A ball or shuttle filled with weft is needed for each color in the design. A design may be laid behind the warp and followed, or it may be made by counting the warp threads to be covered. If a color does not cross the entire web, it is carried to the last point where it is wanted and returned as far as wanted. The new color is started around the warp thread at which the first color was turned back and passed to the last point where it is needed. Several different colors may be in each row of weaving. This and most other weaving problems cannot be appreciated or understood entirely from reading about them but must be worked out on a loom to get the effect.

Single Warp. Single warp is a weave in which the weft encircles each warp thread. See Fig. 12. When wool is used for weft it makes an elastic fabric. To make it firm, a fine binding weft in plain weave is put between strands of the weft encircling the warp. The weft is pushed close together so that the binding does not show.

Tapestry. Tapestry is a weave in which the weft entirely covers the warp both back and front, as it is packed closely. See Fig. 13. A shed entirely across the web is seldom required,

21

Fig. 13. Tapestry weaving. The pattern is held behind the warp with a wide stick. Some of the weft yarn is wound into little bobbinlike balls. A stretcher is being used to keep the woven fabric of even width. In the foreground are: A long pointed flat stick for picking up warp threads. The round stick pointed at each end is used for the same purpose. The comb is used to press the weft close together. The tape measure is useful in checking the length and width of weaving. The other two articles are plastic pick-up shuttles; one has yarn on it.

and the weft is laid in as indicated by a pattern placed behind the warp or followed by counting little squares representing warp threads to be covered by a given color. The work is done in no regular order. A pick-up stick, sometimes called a stylus or a pick-up shuttle, is used to raise the warp to allow the weft to

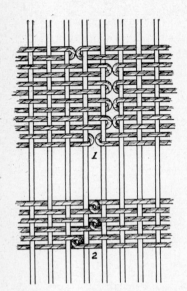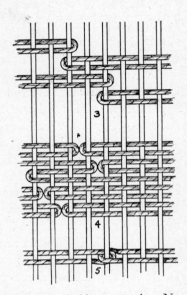

Fig. 14. Diagrams showing how weft is joined in making tapestries. No. 1 — Each weft is turned back at the last warp thread it reaches. When several weft are turned at the same warp, little slits are left in the fabric which have to be sewed together with fine stitches. No. 2 — the weft threads are looped together at the turn between the warp. This results in a slight blending of colors around the edges of figures in the design, while in the method shown in No. 1 there is a sharp distinction between colors. No. 3 — Here the weft is joined around the warp at each turn. This makes a slight ridge where the weft threads meet. No. 4 — The design is planned so each pick is turned at a different warp. No. 5 — The different weft colors are both looped through each other and around the same warp where they meet. Some weavers combine these methods of joining weft, and others use but one style in a single article.

pass through the shed formed. If different colors of yarn are used, there must be several little bobbins or shuttles filled with each. Except for the fact that the weft is turned back and forth at each point where a color changes, tapestry is basically a plain weave packed close together. There are several ways of joining the weft where colors change and of disposing of the ends left in starting and finishing.

23

Tapestries made by different methods are known by different names. Some are called by the names of places where fine tapestries were once made, like arras and gobelin. See Fig. 14.

Woven in one way, little openings are left between the color changes, which later have to be sewed together with fine stitches. Fig. 14, No. 1. This makes a sharp distinction between the colors. Some tapestry weavers leave the ends of weft hanging on the wrong side to avoid thick places resulting from tucking them in between the rows of weft. This method is suitable for upholstery, where the wrong side will not show. Tapestries for other purposes may have the ends carefully tucked in so that they are reversible. Some are made so that there are no little slits to be sewed together. See Fig. 14, Nos. 2, 3, 4, and 5.

Tapestry is usually woven either on a frame or an upright loom because it is easier to follow the design on these. When a frame is used, it should be larger than the finished article. Legs may be attached to the top of the frame by hinges, with loose pins to hold it almost upright as it rests on the lap. See Fig. 15. Legs from a camera tripod are also suited to this purpose, for they can be adjusted to the size of the frame and the height of the lap of the weaver.

Putting on Warp for Tapestry. Strong, smooth warp is best for tapestry. It should be tightly wound around a frame loom. This helps in covering it with weft. See Fig. 16. Spacing and size of warp depend upon the size of weft and the thickness of the cloth desired. Wrapping the warp seven or eight times around a frame will make about fifteen to an inch. One way to space the warp without making a shed is to crochet a row across the warp, taking up one or more threads in each stitch. Tie the beginning and the end of the thread used for crocheting to the sides of the frame. The length needed for crocheting is four times the width. This is pushed to the top of the frame. Repeat the crocheting to space the warp at the bottom of the loom, including the same warp in each stitch. The stitches should be

24

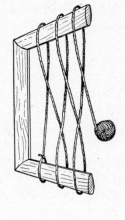

Fig. 15   Fig. 16

Fig. 15. Diagram showing how legs may be attached to a frame loom.
The pins in the hinges may be removed to take off the legs. Fig. 16. A suitable way to warp a frame for tapestry.

quite short and the warp evenly tight all the way across. The
loom is now ready for weaving. An inch or more of plain weaving using warp as weft may be made to help in finishing after
the piece is removed from the loom.

Designs for Tapestry. Select or make a picture pattern. See
Fig. 13. A design with flowing curves is preferable to one with
many vertical straight lines, as this reduces the number of slits
or difficult splicing. The pattern should be distinct and on some
material which will not tear easily, such as architect's tracing
cloth. Other designs may be worked out on cross-ruled paper,
letting each square represent where a weft is to cross the warp.

Tools for Making Tapestry. Plenty of little shuttles of the
pick-up type or little bobbins of yarn, a stylus, and a strong,
pliable stick for holding the pattern in place are needed. The
pliable stick should be about 2½ inches wide, ³⁄₁₆ inch thick,
and 4 or 5 inches longer than the loom is wide. It is used to

hold the pattern under the warp so that it may be followed. The stylus, if used, should be of hardwood, like ash or walnut, that will take a good polish and retain a sharp point. The one illustrated in Fig. 13 is 9 inches long, ⅜ inch in diameter at the center, and tapers to a point at each end. The stylus or the pick-up shuttle is used to lift warp threads for inserting wool, silk, or other weft. Tapestry may or may not be woven entirely across the web at any one time, but the weft must be put in so that it will make a firm material with no horizontal openings. Fig. 14 shows how weft threads may be joined to avoid slits. A purse 7 x 8 inches requires about 50 yards of cotton warp and three 2-ounce skeins of tapestry wool, a 7-inch zipper, a lining 8 x 14 inches, and some stiffening.

Shuttles

The little bobbinlike ball previously mentioned is a useful device when doing finger weaving, or in making tapestries and other fabrics requiring short lengths of a variety of colors or kinds of weft. A shuttle is a better device for putting in long lengths of weft. See Fig. 17, Nos. 4 and 5, and Fig. 18. A simple one for a small loom may be made quickly from a thin piece of wood or stiff cardboard. These are very useful in managing a length of weft which does not have to be passed through a wide shed, and to supplement other shuttles when a great variety of colors is used. A pick-up shuttle of plastic or polished wood may be purchased; having a point, it is also suited to making lace and other weaves in which the warp is picked up a few at a time.

Boatlike shuttles, Fig. 18, are useful in carrying very long lengths of warp and speed up the weaving of most fabrics, as they may be quickly thrown through a wide shed. They come in several sizes, and at least two of these should form a part of the weaving equipment. More are desirable when weaving patterns. The boatlike shuttle carries a bobbin, quill, or spool of

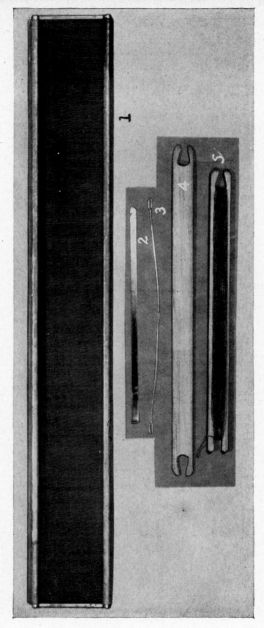

Fig. 17. No. 1 — Reed. No. 2 — Warping hook. No. 3 — Metal heddle. Nos. 4 and 5 — Flat wooden shuttles. (No. 5 has weft wound on it.)

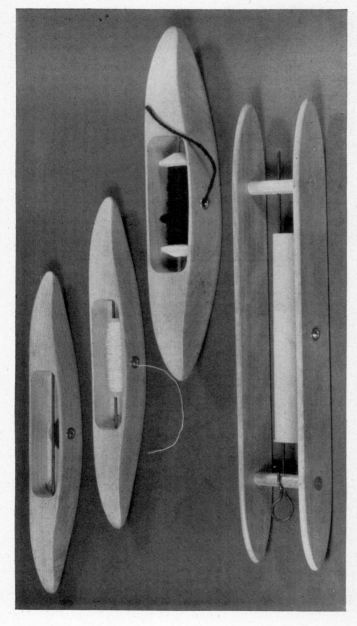

Fig. 18. In the three boat shuttles, a spring holds the pin carrying the bobbin in place. The fourth shuttle has a wire for carrying a bobbin or spool. This may be removed and the weft wound around the shuttle from end to end. This shuttle is useful when coarse, heavy weft is used.

Fig. 19. A small reel used when winding yarn from a ball. A long thin nail driven through the top piece of board is held upright by the heavier piece under it. On this a spool bobbin is placed, and the ball put over the top of it. This avoids getting the yarn fastened around the nail as the ball unwinds. An electric beater may be used as a bobbin winder by putting the bobbin (shown at left) on the spindle. Use a simple overlapping of the thread in starting the bobbin.

weft on a pin so that it unwinds freely as the shuttle goes through the web. A small quill will hold more weft and turn more easily in a shuttle than will a bobbin. Weavers sometimes make their own quills by rolling strong paper on a knitting needle or the spindle of a bobbin winder and fastening it into shape with gummed paper. Some do not fasten it but merely hold it in shape as they start the winding of the weft. Weft is secured to a spool, bobbin, or quill by overlapping the first few windings. See Fig. 19. The weft should never be tied to them. They should be wound firmly and evenly enough to keep the yarn from slipping off and twisting around the pin in the shuttle.

The fourth shuttle in Fig. 17 is designed to carry large amounts of heavy rug material. It is made in two styles, one without and one with a wire for carrying a bobbin. Without the bobbin wire, the weft may be wound around from end to end. This too may be thrown through a shed.

Leash Stick and Strings

As the weaver gains experience, he will feel the need for some way of raising the second warp threads all at once; otherwise, he has to pick them up one or more at a time to put in the weft. A stick to which a leash string, or strings, may be attached is used for this purpose. These are devices that are convenient when some very special group of threads needs to be raised. They are generally used on frame looms without harnesses. See Fig. 1, No. 4, for way to use a leash string.

The string should be of stout cord eight or ten times as long as the group of warp is wide, and is laid under the warp to be raised by the stick while it is held over them. The stick may be a piece of dowel rod ⅜ to ½ inch in diameter and a little longer than the total width of the warp to be raised. The end of the cord is tied to the stick; then a loop of the cord from between the first and second warp to be lifted is pulled up. With the same motion used in putting yarn on a knitting needle, it is secured to the stick, leaving a loop of 3 or more inches. See Fig. 20A. Now, by pulling on the stick the first warp is lifted. To raise the next one, pull up the cord lying between the second and third warp and secure it to the stick, leaving a loop the same length as the first one made. This will raise the second warp in the series. Continue making loops of even length until there is one to lift each warp thread in the set; then tie the cord securely to the stick. When properly put on, the stick will lift the entire set of warp, making a shed that is different from the one made by the shed stick or other devices. With two sheds provided for, one can make all types of over-and-under weaves on a simple loom.

Leash Strings. Leash strings may be inserted for lifting cer-

30

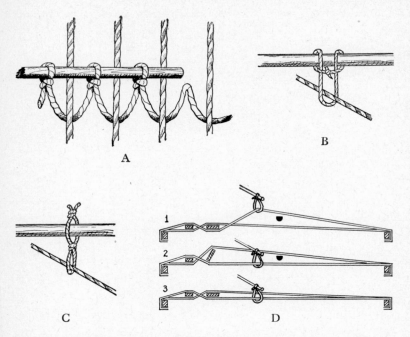

Fig. 20. A. Diagram of method of putting a leash string on rod. B and C. Two ways of making single leash strings. The ends of B are tied and it is looped over the rod. Overhand knots are used in tying C. D shows how the warp threads are raised. No. 1 — The rod and leash raise the warp attached. No. 2 — The shed stick is turned on edge to raise the warp going over it. No. 3 — The leash rod is lying loose on the work. The ♥ mark in the sheds between the warp indicates where the shuttle is put through.

tain warp. They are made by cutting lengths of cord about 4 inches longer than the length needed to make loops. Each cord is then put under a warp thread where needed and tied to a leash stick. Care should be taken in tying them so that all the loops will be of equal length. See Fig. 20B and C.

Use of Shed Stick with Leashes. Weaving with both shed stick and leashes proceeds as follows:

(1) Turn the leash stick on edge, raising the warp that passes over it. While holding it in this position, put the shuttle filled

31

with the weft through the opening or shed formed between the two sets of warp, and then let the shed stick fall back in position.

(2) The weft is now between the two sets of warp and at a slight angle across the web. Taking hold of both ends of the shed stick, draw it against the weft to put it in the desired position straight across the web, and then put the shed stick back in its place at the far end of the loom.

(3) The loops of the leash strings have been pushed against the weft by the shed stick. Take hold of the rod on which they are fastened and, moving it back to place, pull up the warp going through the loops and put the shuttle back through the shed.

(4) Let go the leash rod and grasp the ends of the shed stick, drawing it again against the weft to push it in place beside the other pick of weft, and push the shed stick back.

(5) Repeat these steps until the weaving is finished. See Fig. 20D.

Finishing and Starting New Pieces of Weaving

When a piece of weaving has reached the desired length, it is often a good plan to finish it with an inch of plain weaving. If there is enough warp left on the loom to make another piece, then a thread of colored weft is put in to mark the place for cutting the material apart and the weaving can proceed. If fringe is needed to finish the ends of either or both, enough coarse material, like carpet rags, may be woven in until the warp ends are the length wanted. Should the coarse filler make the end of the weaving seem uneven, it is well to weave in a straight stick such as a dowel rod and start the new weaving after this.

Sometimes a weaver wishes to remove a piece of work before all the warp is used and save it for making other articles. Warp wound around a frame is often so short that removing the work and saving the remaining warp is not practical, but when long lengths are on a loom, a piece may be removed as follows: At

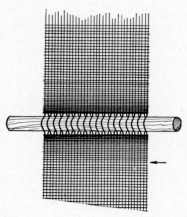

Fig. 21. Diagram showing end of a finished length of cloth before it is removed from the loom. The firm weaving above the arrow is to hold a dowel and the ends of the warp so that they may be tied to the cloth beam. This and the tabby beginning for the new piece of cloth must be made before cutting away a piece of material. The cloth is cut at the point indicated by the arrow. The dowel not only furnishes a means of attaching the web to the cloth beam but keeps the ends of the warp straight. Otherwise, a considerable length of cloth should be woven and left on the loom, when a piece is to be cut off.

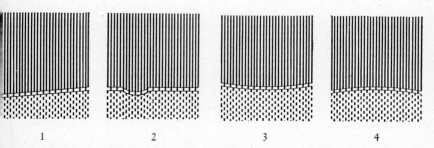

| 1 | 2 | 3 | 4 |

Fig. 22. Diagrams showing weaving difficulties. No. 1 — Edge of web is slanting or pulled out of line in winding on the roller or in starting. Try rewinding to make even. No. 2 — Unevenness caused by a variation in the tightness of the warp due to uneven tension when tying the warp ends, bunching of material on the rollers, or when two kinds of warp are combined and one is more elastic or coarser than the other. No. 3 — The warp in the selvage is too tight. No. 4 — Warp in selvage is too loose.

the end of a piece to be taken off, weave, beating down tightly, an inch or more of tabby; put in a dowel rod and weave another inch, beating it to make a firm cloth. Cut off the piece at the point indicated by the arrow, Fig. 21, and tie the dowel securely to the near end of the loom and proceed with the weaving.

Some Difficulties Found in Weaving

Loops. Little loops in the selvage and other defects show that the weft is not pulled tightly enough. When pulled too tight the cloth is narrowed; this can be corrected by putting it in more loosely. Most weft should be put in as loosely as it can be without leaving loops and knots. When not kept at an even tension, one part of the finished cloth may be narrower than another.

Pulled Edge. The edge of the web may be pulled out of shape when winding finished work on the cloth beam in order to bring more warp into place for weaving. Try rewinding. This difficulty may also be caused by beating harder at one side than the other. Take care to beat evenly.

Unevenness in Edge of Web. The cause of unevenness in the edge of the web is likely to be a variation in the tightness of the warp or an uneven start. See Fig. 22. Use a straight rod to help make a straight start. Retie the warp ends to make them even in tension. If the cause is a loose thread or a second retieing is not practical, tie a weight to it to make the same tension as the others. If quite a group are loose, put a piece of paper under them to make them more taut.

Uneven Spacing. Uneven spacing of the weft is due to uneven beating — that is, light and heavy. Warp spaced too wide in relation to the weft has a tendency to make it slip. See Fig. 23.

A bad start may cause unevenness in the weaving, as does uneven tension of warp. It may also be caused during the process of moving the woven cloth onto or toward its beam by some warp threads catching and pulling unevenly or because of bunches of material on the cloth beam. This latter difficulty may be overcome by laying paper or sticks the width of

34

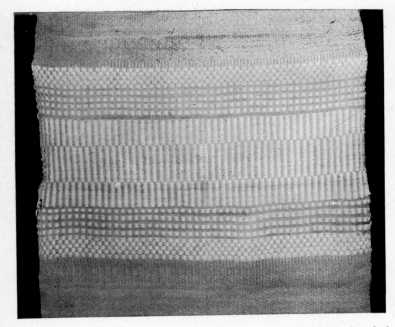

Fig. 23. Near the ends there is uneven spacing of the weft in the cloth due to uneven beating and some slippage. This material was woven on a twill threading. The center is made by alternating a heavy pattern weft with a tabby weft like the warp. Treadling is explained on pages 45, 46.

the beam between it and the warp or the cloth as it is being wound on the beam.

How to Handle Long Lengths of Warp on a Board or Frame Loom

Having mastered the rudiments of weaving, one may go a few steps further on the frame loom and provide for making a long runner or a number of articles on one length of warp. The device which will fill this function of keeping long warp in order and in a manageable state corresponds to the warp and cloth rollers or beams on table and floor looms. It is made of two

35

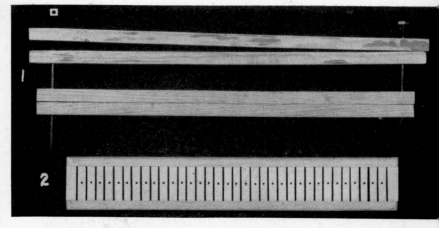

Fig. 24. No. 1 — Pairs of sticks, held together with bolts, used for holding long lengths of warp on a frame loom. No. 2 — Combined heddle and beater or reed for a frame loom.

pairs of sticks. See Fig. 24, No. 1. The ends of the warp are clamped between the sticks to keep them parallel and are tied to keep them from pulling out. One pair is used to roll up the warp to a length that will go around the frame; the other is used for rolling the cloth when it is made. The warp is stretched around the frame and the pairs of sticks are tied or bolted together at the back of the loom. The ties or nuts are adjusted to give the warp the proper tension. If the warp is not evenly tight when the sticks are parallel, the warp ends must be untied where they are loose, pulled to an even tension, and retied. As soon as the cross and warp sticks and the leashes are in place, the loom is ready for weaving.

To dispose of the finished material and bring more warp into use, the ties or bolts are undone. The cloth is rolled on one and some warp unrolled from the other; then the ties or bolts are replaced. The loom is laid face down on the floor or on a

Fig. 25. Warp face weave made by pushing warp, on which the tabby weave in Fig. 2 was made, close together so that it covers the weft.

table while this is being done, for in this position the shed stick and leashes will not get out of place. This device is very helpful on small looms used for making bead bands, belting, and other articles too long for the loom. As indicated above, care must be taken in winding warp on a beam for any loom so that each strand will be the same tension and length at all times from roller to roller; and the rollers must be kept parallel to each other. A fully equipped frame loom is a useful supplement to the table or foot-power loom, so nothing is lost in preparing one. On such a loom of suitable dimensions, rugs and other heavy materials of considerable size may be woven.

Variety of Weaves Suggested in This Chapter

The variety of weaves the weaver should be able to make on any loom now include:

Fig. 26. No. 1 — Inlay. No. 2 — Inlay and a knotted end.

(1) Plain or tabby weaves, in which the sheds are made of alternating warp and the weft beaten in so that warp and weft show equally. See Fig. 2.

38

(2) Inlay of contrasting color laid in with the tabby weft to make spots or little figures in the fabric. See Fig. 26, Nos. 1 and 2.

(3) Basket weave, in which the warp is lifted in groups of two or more and the same number of weft put in one after the other. This is beaten so that warp and weft show equally. Three of the pot holders in Fig. 8 are modifications of this weave.

(4) Weft face weaves. In these, the warp is held taut enough so that the weft can be beaten in to entirely cover the warp. See Figs. 13, the background of 43, No. 1, and 47.

(5) Warp face weaves in which the warp are placed so close together that the weft will not show between them. The warp must be somewhat loose and the weft drawn tight enough to keep the warp threads close to each other. See Figs. 25 and 48.

(6) Darning weaves. Figs. 4 and 6.

(7) Tapestries. Fig. 14.

(8) Single-warp finger weave. Fig. 12.

(9) Indian tie, also a finger weave. Fig. 10.

(10) Sumak. Fig. 11.

Combinations of all the above are used by every weaver.

CHAPTER III

Weaving on Table and Floor Looms

THE machine has extensively superseded the hand loom in making all but the most costly fabrics. A fabric that must be woven as well as weaving can be done, without consideration of cost, however, is made on a hand loom. The money outlay and room required for an old-time, large, stationary loom, which looks most intriguing, has hampered the art of weaving in homes in modern times. But newer models are available which are much less cumbersome and which can be warped and operated by one person alone. Some of them fold and may be stored in a comparatively small space. See Fig. 27.

The choice between a table and a floor loom is a matter of finance, and the extent and type of weaving for which it is intended. Wide looms with warp beams divided into sections can be warped by one person, as can table looms which are narrower. A person working alone will also need the following: a device for winding yarn on bobbins, Fig. 19, spools, or quills; something to hold balls, spools, and bobbins when putting warp on the loom and winding the bobbins, Fig. 28; a separator to keep the warp in order during the process of warping (see card in Fig. 28); a stretcher to keep the cloth even in width, Fig. 13; shuttles, scissors, tape measure, pins, and a few assorted needles.

First Costs

A frame loom may be made with no outlay of money or it

Fig. 27. Folding floor loom ready for storage. The crank at the side is removable. The treadles, in this model, connect directly with the frames carrying the heddles. *Loom Craft Studio, Wilmington, Ohio.*

may cost up to $5.00. A table loom may be homemade and cost up to $10.00. Purchased ready-made, table looms vary in price from around $5.00 up to $50.00. The cost of a new foot-power loom starts around $35.00 and goes up as high as $300.00, depending on the width, construction and other factors. Home weavers with an ambition to turn out a quantity of very small articles with a ready-made table loom will probably invest around $50.00 in equipment. Those who desire to make a greater variety of fabrics, including wider materials, will probably invest $100.00 for a floor outfit, because besides the loom it is desirable to have the accessories mentioned previously.

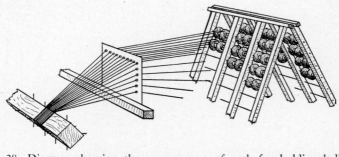

Fig. 28. Diagram showing the arrangement of rack for holding balls or spools of warp, warp guide or separator attached to back beam of loom, and sectional warp beam, on which the warp is wound. Some guides have parts used to regulate the tension of the warp as it goes on the loom. When using the simpler ones, this may be done by holding the warp in the hand between the rack and the guide.

Table Looms — Upright and Horizontal

Upright or Morris Type. A table loom of the type developed by William Morris, nineteenth-century artist, printer, and furniture designer, is one that stands on end. See Fig. 29. The back beam, breast beam, and two side pieces form the frame, which is held together by pegs. Through the ends of the two beams, No. 3, the warp and cloth are wound on rollers, Nos. 4 and 5. A removable nail prevents each from turning while the weaving is in process. It can easily be removed to turn the roller. Instead of leash strings, this loom has a harness composed of heddles held in frames which are moved forward and backward by rotating rollers to which they are attached by straps, No. 2. A board at each side holds the rollers in place. Sometimes the upright sides of the loom are extended between breast beam and base; then it becomes a floor loom.

In order to understand the operation of any loom, you must examine it. You cannot learn weaving without materials to experiment with. But a description will help you decide what you want to try first.

The Morris type of loom is desirable for making tapestries,

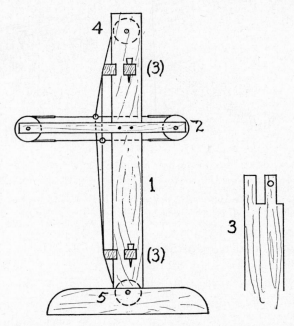

Fig. 29. Diagram of side view of Wm. Morris type loom. No. 1 — Lower
side piece. No. 2 — Harness. No. 3 — Beams. Nos. 4 and 5 — Rollers. This
loom can be taken apart for compact storage, as it is held together by four
pins in the ends of the back and breast beams, No. 3. Four small bolts hold
the harness for making sheds in the warp to the sides of the frame. The
total height of the table model is 26 inches and of the floor model 65
inches.

knotted rugs, and some other heavy fabrics which are too variable
in design to be woven only by the insertion of weft in sheds
of warp. The heddles, No. 2, aid in making tabby which forms
the foundation for knotting and picture weaving. The design
is usually fastened behind the warp threads, so that it may be
seen through them. See Figs. 13 and 29.

The general procedure for weaving on this loom is to make
an inch or more of tabby, moving the frames of heddles to
make the sheds. Next bring the warp to a neutral position — that

Fig. 30. Diagrams showing how knots for tufting or making a pile are tied. 1, Ghiordes, 2, Senna, and 3, Single warp knot.

is, without a shed — put in the pattern weft or filler as described for tapestry, and sumak weaves or a row or two of knots or loops of weft picked up between the warp. Then weave some more tabby to hold them in place. The number of rows of plain weaving used for binding varies from one to eight with the weight of filler or knotting yarn and the texture desired. The knots used include Ghiordes, Senna, and single warp. See Fig. 30. Knitting needles may be used to pick up the weft to form other loops or knots. See Fig. 63.

These knots and loops are not only used in making rugs but ornamental textured draperies and in making fluffy edges for pillow covers. See Fig. 26, No. 2. A small sample should be made before attempting to make large articles, in order to find a proper balance between binding and pile.

Horizontal Type. A table loom is adequate for small-scale weaving. It is generally less than 24 inches wide, which makes cloth somewhat narrower. Being small, it is easily moved about. Such looms derive their name from the fact that they are intended to be set on a table. Both the horizontal and the Morris types can be converted into floor looms by attaching legs and treadles. See Fig. 31.

The horizontal table loom is composed of a frame consisting of a breast beam at the near end and a back beam at the far end. There is a roller under each beam, one for cloth and one for warp. The main difference between this and the looms already

44

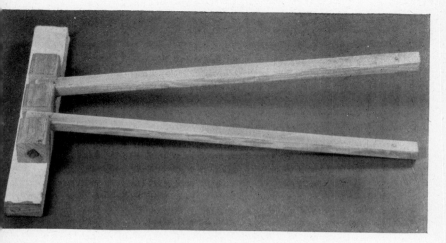

Fig. 31. Homemade treadles for a two-frame table loom. A long bolt acts as a hinge or pivot for the sticks forming the treadles. A cord through the other end of each treadle is tied to a frame of heddles. When a treadle is pressed down, the frame attached is pulled down.

described is that there is a reed used for spacing the warp and for beating it into place, instead of a shed stick and comb. See Figs. 32, 33, and 34.

Reed and Beater

A reed used as a beater is an essential in hand looms. It may be made at home, but one from some firm selling weaving devices is likely to be smoother, more accurate, and stronger. The spaces between the wires or flat bars of metal comprising the reed are called dents. The number of dents to an inch and its length are used in describing a reed. They vary in width but the common one is about 4 inches. For very coarse materials, six dents to an inch are suitable; for finer work, 12, 15, 16, and 20 are the most common numbers seen. See Figs. 17, No. 1, 24, No. 2, and 32.

The reed on a table loom or a floor loom is held in a frame with long arms. The ends of the arms are attached to the frame

Fig. 32. Table loom with heddle frames in neutral position, the warp going straight from beam to beam. Some string heddles have been inserted. The strings on the beater indicate the center and other points in a pattern to aid in warping. Before raising it on the supporting blocks shown, to permit the insertion of pieces of tape and a bar to help draw each frame down as the other was lifted, this loom would not work. The warp also goes through the reed in its frame, which is used for spacing the warp and as a beater.

of the loom so that the reed in its frame may be easily swung to the edge of the web to push the weft in place. At the bottom of the reed, the frame holding it is rather wide to make a shuttle race.

How to Use the Reed. When using the reed as a beater, especially on large looms, lay the fingers back of the top to swing it toward the weaver, letting go before it strikes the edge of the

Fig. 33. Front view of table loom. Considerable adjustment had to be made to make this one work well and to protect the weaver from being hurt by the ratchet wheels. One shed is open.

weft. This avoids jerking the body and makes weaving a much easier process. As soon as the reed hits the web, be ready to swing the beater back with the thumbs. This method of handling the beater will speed up weaving without tiring the weaver.

Heddles, Frames of Heddles, and Harness

As in the upright looms, heddles strung in frames are used on horizontal looms for raising the warp instead of a shed stick and leashes. See Fig. 35. Some writers call the heddles in their frames "harnesses." One writer on weaving says that in Amer-

47

Fig. 34. Back view of the same table loom. The other shed is open. Note
the position of the handle that turns the top roller.

ican usage the frames on which the heddles are strung are called
"harnesses," and that in European books "a harness is a different
matter." Webster says that in weaving the harness is the "part
of a loom comprising the heddles, with their means of support
and motion, by which the threads of warp are alternately raised
and depressed." In accepting Webster's definition, we understand
that the heddle frames are only a part of the harness, which includes the rollers, pulleys, levers or lams, and their connecting
ropes, straps or chains which move the heddles and support them.
Hand looms are equipped with various arrangements of the parts

48

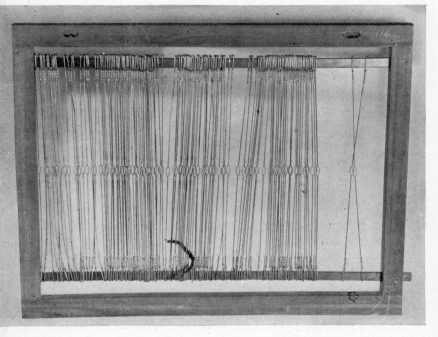

Fig. 35. A frame of heddles taken from the table loom illustrated. The heddles are strung on metal bars which are held in place by small pins. One is being removed to uncross the two heddles at the end. Crossed heddles give trouble in weaving. There are 116 heddles in this frame. The bit of yarn marks the center one.

forming the harness which speed the making of sheds in the warp. The important quality in a harness is that it operates smoothly and make sheds wide enough to pass a fair-sized boat or a rug shuttle through.

A table loom should be equipped with at least two frames of heddles to make two sheds. Four frames are desirable, in order to make twills and many patterns. Some looms have more. An increase in the number of sheds makes possible the weaving of

49

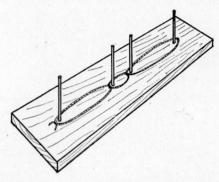

Fig. 36. Diagram of a string heddle on a heddle board.

more patterns, but has little effect on the number of articles to be made.

How Heddles Are Made. Heddles are strung on rods, usually in a frame. There is a loop at each end to hold the heddle on the rods, and there is one in the center, called an eye, through which one warp thread is passed. See Figs. 17, No. 3, and 35. It is best to have a heddle for each warp thread. Ready-made heddles are of two kinds — those made of wire and those made of flat metal. If flat heddles are used, great care must be taken when stringing them so that the eyes are all turned in the same direction.

One should also be careful when stringing any heddles on the bars not to cross them. See Fig. 35. When crossed heddles are found, they should be removed and strung properly.

Directions for Making Heddles of Cord. Occasionally a weaver needs a few heddles to fill in missing ones in a frame or to supplement his supply. A good heddle may be made from hard-twist No. 8/4 carpet warp, fish line, or other strong cord, cut in even 24-inch lengths to make 10-inch heddles. These will be improved if dipped in a pan of hot beeswax and then wiped dry. Construct a heddle board using large nails, Fig. 36, and note how the ties are made. The knots used should be square knots, and one person

50

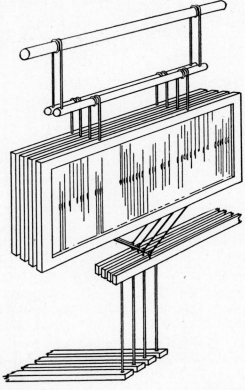

Fig. 37. Diagram of one type of harness for a loom. The frames of heddles are hung from rollers and attached to lams below, which are hinged to the side of the loom frame. The lams are moved by the treadles below them.

should tie all the heddles needed to assure their being of even length.

Number of Heddles Required for Plain Weaving. An equal number of heddles should be on each of the heddle frames used for tabby weaving. When four or more frames of heddles are used, they should be threaded so that half the threads may be raised at each pick. A pick is one shot or throw of the shuttle

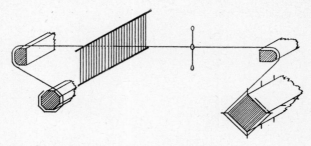

Fig. 38. Diagram showing correct position for a single warp across a loom when no shed is being formed. Cloth beam is at left, warp beam at right.

through a shed. For some pattern weaving, more heddles are needed in one frame than another.

Adjusting the Heddle Frames and Harness. Frames holding heddles must all hang at the same height and level from end to end in a loom. Pairs of them should lift together in unison as wanted, and the heddle eyes should be on a level with a line across the loom when in a neutral position. See Fig. 37. A warp passing over the back beam from the warp beam through the heddle eye in front of it and over the breast beam must be level from beam to beam — that is, neither pulled up or down by the heddle eyes when in this position. See Fig. 38.

When threading a loom with warp wound on the back beam be sure the warp is put around the back beam as illustrated in Fig. 38. Test the loom by raising the heddles in the frames by hand or by pressing the treadles in rotation, to see that all the heddle eyes which move upward are on a line almost to the full height of the reed, and that those which move downward are all on a line with or slightly below the top of the shuttle race, which forms the bottom of the reed. This is essential. If the sheds are not wide enough for the shuttle to travel across, its passage will be impeded and the harness must be adjusted to provide a good shed in the proper location. Sometimes ropes forming a part of the harness may stretch or they may shrink due to dampness in the air; if so, they may need adjusting.

Suggestions for Beginners

Some would-be weavers are discouraged if at first they attempt to set up a complicated or an original pattern on a fully equipped loom. Once experiments in weaving have been tried on simple frame looms or on hand looms that have been properly warped for them, their enthusiasm may carry them on to preparing their own four- or eight-harness looms, and the production of original designs. Those who persevere and learn weaving progressively understand what they are doing and derive much pleasure from it. They know how to make good selvages and cloth of even texture which keeps its shape.

Materials. The materials used for weaving are almost unlimited and may consist of wool, cotton, silk, rayon, nylon, ramie, chenille, bouclé, spun glass, cellophane, reed, raffia, straw, and so forth.

Loom Sizes. The width of articles and material made is limited by the width of the loom used. Their length is limited only by the length of the warp prepared and the size roll it makes. Those interested in making a great variety of articles will find a 42-inch wide loom most satisfactory. It is not too large to operate when making small things and permits making cloth wide enough for curtains, card-table covers, luncheon cloths, and dress goods that will cut to advantage. A 32-inch loom makes cloth that has to be seamed or have borders added to make it wide enough for some of these articles. Looms over 50 inches wide are harder to operate, and some weavers find difficulty in passing shuttles through the shed. When wide looms are used, fly shuttles are desirable.

Fly Shuttles. A fly shuttle is thrown by a mechanical device and not by hand. It runs across the shuttle race into boxes at each side of the loom. A lever or some other device makes it go back and forth as desired. Those used by amateurs carry only one shuttle, and so a fly-shuttle loom is less flexible than one without this device. Professional hand weavers sometimes use a loom equipped with a number of fly shuttles. These require expert care and skill to operate successfully.

Amount of Warp Required. When putting warp on a loom, an extra yard for every five must be allowed in length, because length is taken up in the process of weaving and in shrinkage when the cloth has been removed. Also, enough extra length must be allowed to fasten the warp to aprons or tapes on the warp and cloth beams, and to get it evenly spaced by means of weaving in straight rods and strips of cloth first, and to hold it in position. This length varies with the type of loom, but means that if a piece of cloth 5 yards long is to be made on a hand loom, the warp on the loom must be 6 to 7 yards long. Board and frame looms may require a greater proportion of warp length to the length of the finished article. The waste is less when the double sticks, Fig. 24, No. 1, are used to hold it in place. Warp may be saved by care in attaching and removing material. New warp may be added — that is, tied to old warp on the loom — and effect another economy.

Shrinkage and Warpage. While cloth is on the loom, it is stretched lengthwise. Therefore, when taken off it may measure as much as 3 inches per yard shorter. This shrinkage must be taken into account when measuring material on a loom and in planning finished articles. It also slightly changes the shape of designs. See Fig. 39.

Economies. Many short lengths of yarn may be used as weft when weaving small articles such as pillow covers, scarves, table and place mats, covers for pocketbooks, bags, and squares which may be sewed together in various patterns to make bed spreads. Also, braids, bands, and fringe for trimmings may be made from them, as well as knotted rugs and table runners.

Today, the beginner can get his material for warp wound

Fig. 39. Two towels woven alike, before and after washing. Note shrinkage.

in balls or on bobbins in ten-cent and department stores. They are easier for the lone weaver to manage than yarn in skeins. For the quickest method of putting warp on the beam, it should be on spools or bobbins. A person with a winder can quite easily make as many bobbins as required. A household electric beater may be used if a bobbin winder is not available. With a sufficient number of warp ends, the balls, spools, or bobbins may either be put on a spool rack, Fig. 28, or on large nails driven through a board.

Warping a Loom. Putting the warp threads on a loom incorrectly makes trouble for beginners. Each warp thread must follow a path parallel to those on either side of it, and, while doing this, pass through a heddle eye and a dent in the reed. If long, it must be rolled on the warp beam to keep it in order. See Fig. 38. The beginner should start by using comparatively short lengths of warp. Warp up to 3½ yards long is not difficult to manage. On a table loom, which is narrow, this may make four table place mats; or on a 36-inch floor loom a card table cover and four napkins to match. By the time this much warp is used, the weaver may want to try a different kind. A new warp may be tied to each of the warp ends left in the loom if the same threading is satisfactory.

Two Principal Ways of Putting on Warp. There are two ways to put on warp: one from the front and the other from the back. Both are used by many weavers. The warp started from the front is carried from the bobbins on a rack, through a guide set near or attached to the breast beam, through the dents in the reed, then through the heddle eyes according to the pattern chosen, and attached to the tape or apron on the warp beam on which it is wound. The other end is tied to the cloth beam.

The warp started at the back of the loom is carried from bobbins on a rack through a guide set near or attached to the back beam, and wound on the warp beam. When the correct length is on the beam, the ends of the warp are secured in proper order by making a cross or by adhesive paper or clamps, from which they are threaded through the heddle eyes and then the reed and attached to the cloth beam. A colored string of the desired length threaded the same as the warp, but clear of it, may be used as a measure during the winding. If a counter is provided with the loom, it will measure the warp for you.

Warp Beams. Some warp beams are large enough in diameter so you can measure the warp by counting the turns they make, one turn measuring up to a yard at a time, while others are little larger than a broom handle. Some are divided in sections. See Fig. 40. Sections are an advantage on wide looms, for it is easier

Fig. 40. Folding loom with sectional warp beam. Rolling lams above the treadles form a part of the harness of this model. There are pulleys in the topcastle. *Loom Craft Studio, Wilmington, Ohio.*

to put long warp on in them and not so many spools are required on the rack. A section usually holds enough warp for 2 inches of the reed, so rarely does one need more than eighty bobbins at a time. Other beams may be converted into sectional ones, and some looms come with two beams, one of each type, which may be interchanged. The beams of a small loom may be treated as one section or filled by halves or quarters.

57

A loom having a warp beam divided in sections should have it placed low enough so that no thread will be brought down tight over a peg or other divider as a heddle is lowered; for when this happens a warp thread may break or be stretched, causing bad places in the woven cloth.

Counters for Looms. There are a number of different counters for looms. The measuring string has been mentioned. Another is a mark on the frame of the loom so each beam turn may be counted as the handle passes this mark. The difficulty here is that interruptions cause the weaver to forget the number of turns. A simple measure is a bolt, in which threads are cut the full length. This is inserted in the end of the beam axle and turns with it. One turn of the beam turns the bolt once. An iron bar with a hole in it is hung on the bolt and the inside edge fits between the threads. As the beam is turned, the bar is pushed along until it comes to the end and falls off. It can be set at the proper place to fall off when the desired number of turns have been made.

Warp Guides. A warp separator or guide is a device for keeping the warp threads in order and of fairly even tension as they come from their spools or balls to the loom. One may be bought or homemade. The homemade ones consist of holes punched in a heavy card or piece of metal. See Fig. 28. Hardware cloth may serve as a guide and some people use an extra reed. Warp ends are put through the guide in the order they are to be threaded in the loom, and they must be kept in this order until they are attached to the proper beam. Special instructions come with a manufactured guide. When warping is from the back and a sufficient length of warp is in a section of the beam, that remaining on the bobbins is cut between the guide and the beam, so that it is ready to fill the next section.

Measuring Length of Warp. If the loom is warped from the front, the yarn may be measured on a warping board, Fig. 41, a cross being made as illustrated to keep it in order, or shorter

58

lengths up to 5 yards can lie on the floor and stay in fairly good order. Another method is to put the warp through a guide directly from the balls; then thread through the reed and heddles and attach it to the warp beam. Do not wind until all the heddles to be used are filled. This warp is measured with a tape or yardstick after it is pulled through the guide and before entering the reed and heddles. It is now cut and the ends left are ready to be be put into the dents and heddles. The reed also acts as a warp guide, so this is an efficient way to warp a loom without a sectional beam.

Planning Groups of Warp Thread. Sections on manufactured beams are intended to hold enough warp to thread two inches of the reed. Count the sections and plan the number of warp to go in each. The warp is usually centered in the reed and distributed evenly on each side. If there is a shortage or excess of threads for one side or the other, this should be in the sections at the ends of the beam. Start with the required number of spools on the spool rack to be put in each of the center sections. Later, if sections require more or less spools, they may be added to or removed from the rack.

See that all unwind in the same direction. Wind warp slowly and take care to make it lie flat in the sections or on the beam. Holding the warp between the guide and the spools helps to make an even tension. Avoid mounding or "piling" the warp in the center, as the threads on top will be longer than those on the sides when they are unwound for weaving and there will be difficulty with tight and loose threads in the web.

Keep warp ends in order for threading. When warping a loom from the back, the yarn must be cut after it is wound on the warp beam and before it is threaded through the heddles. Some looms come fitted with wooden clamps for holding the ends in order, while on others adhesive tape is used. By these means a cross need not be maintained, as in the old style warping of looms. When the correct length of warp is in a section, fasten

59

the clamp, or place adhesive tape 10 inches from where the warp is to be cut. Take care that the tape holds them in the order they come through the guide. Cut the warp and tie it to the peg at the side nearest the center of the beam. Wind the remaining sections, doing those nearest the center first. When starting to fill a section, reset the counter, or begin to count the turns of the beam so the same length of warp is in each section. Any empty sections should be at the ends.

There are other methods of preparing warp and putting it on a loom but most of them require a helper.

Threading Heddles on the Loom with Sectional Beam. When all the warp is on the beam, threading may begin. The warp in each section should be threaded into the heddles and dents directly ahead of it. This brings the warp across the loom from beam to beam without being pulled to one side or the other. If threads are out of line they become looser than the others and give trouble as the work progresses. Untie the central group of warp from its peg. Care must be taken to keep it in the order it comes from the guide, and do not let it turn or roll over. Take the thread nearest the center of the loom from between its clamp or piece of gummed paper and put it through its proper heddle eye according to the pattern being followed. Do the same with the others in the order they come from the paper.

Some persons thread all heddles and then the reed, while others prefer to thread both heddle and reed at the same time.

Threading the Reed. Patterns indicate the threading of the reed by the words single, double, sley single, or sley double, or by a certain number to an. inch, as 10, 20, or 30. Single or sley single means one warp to a dent, and double or sley double, two to a dent. Should a reed have twenty dents to an inch and the instructions read 15, then one dent in every four would be left empty. If thirty are indicated there would be two threads in each alternate dent and single threads in the others. It is advisable to thread fifteen dents double rather than thirty dents single, as there is less wear on the warp in double threading, especially when a soft warp like wool is being used.

Warping Hook. Warp threads are pulled through the reed and heddle eyes with a hook. See Fig. 17, No. 2. This may be purchased, or made by cutting a hook in one end of a thin, flat piece of metal 8 to 15 inches long. An old clock spring makes a good hook.

How a Cross Is Made in Yarn. A cross is made by winding yarn back and forth around four or more pegs. The yarn is tied to the first one and carried in and out past the two in the center, turned around the fourth, and brought back past the center ones on the opposite side from those on which it first passed; then back to the first peg, where it is turned around to follow the path made by the beginning thread. These steps are followed until there are as many warp threads as needed. There is a cross made by the yarn where it passes first on one side and then on the other of the center peg. A string tied around the warp each side of the cross will keep the yarn in the order it was put around the pegs. See Fig. 41.

Checking the Threading. After threading about an inch of a repeat pattern, it should be checked to see that no error has been made. If one is found, it should be corrected immediately. Mistakes in threading change the pattern or appearance of the finished fabric and are likely to ruin the design. After the threads have been correctly pulled through the heddles and reed, they are tied to the warp or the cloth beam, depending on which direction it was threaded. The tying is done in small groups so that it will be spaced evenly across the loom. After all have been tied, they should be tested by laying the hand on the web of warp to see if all threads are of even tension. If not, they are retied until even. As this is done, be sure that each strand goes straight across the loom and is not caught anywhere nor crossed with another thread. When the tying is completed, move the frames of heddles in rotation, making the different

Fig. 41. Warping board. The short pieces of yarn are looped around the two crosses to hold the warp in the order it was put on the warping board.

sheds, and check each. A thread in the middle of a shed indicates something is wrong. If an error is found, trace the thread back and correct. Next test the pattern by putting in a few rows of coarse yarn or carpet rags, and check again for errors. Use carpet rags, waste yarn, or string, and weave until the warp is evenly spaced. Next put in a few picks of plain weaving. Be sure the edge of the web is straight, but if it is not it may be made so by weaving in a small dowel rod. Check for irregularities in design and correct if necessary. When the weaving is perfect, the loom is ready.

Use of Boat Shuttle. When using a boatlike shuttle in weaving, it is thrown through the shed with a quick movement of the wrist, and caught at the other end. The beater is then thrown against the edge of the fabric to press the weft in place. The positions of the heddle frames are changed, making a new shed, and the beater again brought down against the weft and pushed away to make room for the shuttle to be thrown again. The above process is repeated in most weaving. Care must be taken so that the floor of the shed rests firmly on the bottom of the reed frame, which is sometimes called the shuttle race. When ready to throw the shuttle, the fingers should be underneath and the thumb on top to control the tension of the bobbin. A weaving "pick" or "shot" is a throw of a shuttle across the loom. "Pick" is sometimes used to mean the number of weft or filling threads to an inch. It is also used to mean the blow which drives the shuttle. The speed of a loom is reckoned as so many picks per minute.

Selvages. The sides of woven cloth must be at right angles to the reed and kept the width of the threading. If they draw in too much, the warp at the sides will become worn and will break from friction in beating. Drawing in at the sides indicates that the weft is being drawn too tight. It should be as loose as possible yet not leave loops on the edge of the material. The use to which material is to be put determines the care with which the selvage is made. See Fig. 42. Upholstery material is better if the ends of the weft are left hanging. The selvage will be out of sight, and, to avoid bulkiness, can be made thinner by not tucking in the warp ends, if the strength of the fabric is not sacrificed. See Fig. 43.

Selvages on towels should be made with care to avoid loops, and the end of each weft thread tucked back into the edge. In some weaving, an extra strong thread or two of warp may be at the edge of the selvage to give it strength.

How to Add a Weft Thread. Open a shed and start a weft thread by holding the end between the fingers, as the shuttle is thrown through the shed. Winding the end around the little finger is another way of holding it. After the first weft is in

Fig. 42. Card table cover and napkins to match. Woven on a loom without changing the warp. These need carefully made selvages. The two napkins, each being half as wide as the cover, are woven side by side, using a shuttle for each.

Fig. 43. Three hand-woven fabrics intended for chair seat covers. All were made on the same threading of warp as the luncheon set in Fig. 42. In No. 1, the weft of wool entirely covers the cotton warp. In No. 2, a variety of treadlings was used and the warp shows through a little. No. 1 and 2 are reversible, being similar on both sides. In No. 3, the wool weft is kept on the face of the material where it covers the warp, while the warp is much in evidence on the back. This is a brocade weave.

place and the next shed made, turn the end of the weft under a few warp threads and proceed with the weaving.

When the end of a weft thread is reached, the end that remains which will not make a complete pick across the web is left hanging out at the selvage until the next shed is opened, when it is turned in the width of the selvage. The new weft is then put in and the following shed opened. Into this the end of the new weft is turned and the weaving continued. The two ends are then cut close to the fabric. Should a weft be added that is a different type or color, its end may have to go into the same shed that it crosses, so it must be wrapped around the outside thread of the selvage before being turned into the shed.

Adding New Warp. If the same threading is desired for another piece of material requiring different warp, the new warp ends may be tied to the ends of those already in the loom and drawn through the heddles and the reed. This may be done either from the front or the back.

When tied at the front, the reed may serve as a guide and all the warp wound onto the warp beam at one time. This method is particularly well adapted to looms having undivided warp beams.

When tied at the back, the warp on the loom is used until only enough is left for holding it in place through the heddle eyes and for tying. The warp is cut evenly and knotted loosely to hold it in place while the beam is warped. When the warp is on the beam, then the new warp ends are tied to the old ones in consecutive order.

Why Warp Threads Break. Warp threads break because they are too tight, worn by friction, caught in the shuttle, or caught on some part of the loom. A break should be mended immediately. If it occurs between the reed and the fabric, an extra length of yarn is tied to the broken end coming from the warp beam and pulled forward to the same tension as the rest of the warp. It is fastened with a pin to the fabric. The end from the cloth is pulled back over the edge of the cloth. When the weaving has proceeded far enough to hold the warp in place, the pin is removed and the two ends carefully darned into the fabric and the thread cut. See Fig. 44.

If, in breaking, a thread snaps out of the reed and heddle, the empty dent and heddle eye are found; the rest of the warp is pushed apart on either side; the broken thread is picked up at the warp beam, threaded through the heddle and the dent, then pinned to the cloth. Care must be taken to keep it in its proper path so it will not cross other warp threads.

A piece of warp long enough to finish the article on which the weaver is working may be added to a broken thread and

Fig. 44. (Warp runs sidewise in this display.) This sample of material was woven on a twill threading of the warp. Fig. 23 shows another pattern developed on a twill threading. The loose warp end needs to be darned into the fabric. Note loose thread to be cut.

pulled over the back beam, where it is weighted to give it the proper tension while the weaving proceeds. When this piece of weaving is completed, the original warp end will have become long enough to use in beginning the next piece.

Variety of Weaves in This Chapter

The variety of weaves in this chapter has not increased, but the weaver should be able to use them efficiently in making many more and larger articles than he made on the frame. These will include such articles as towels with stripes in colored weft, or inlaid borders and monograms; material for covering chair seats and backs; place mats; small luncheon sets; scarves; and baby blankets, in weaves requiring two sheds. See Fig. 45. He will also have learned to accomplish more per hour.

CHAPTER IV

Design and Draft Reading

D ESIGN is the result of careful planning.

(1) It is developed by the kind of yarn used, its size, color and luster, and whether it is tightly or loosely twisted. A well-twisted thread is strong but it is harder and smaller for its weight than one loosely twisted. Strong thread is needed for warp. The weft may vary greatly in strength. Some fabrics contain a variety of either weft, warp, or both. Cloth must be constructed so that it will serve the purpose for which it is intended. Pot holders must be thick and glass curtains thin or lacy. The strength of cloth depends not only on the strength of the threads used but also on the number of times per inch they are interlaced with one another.

(2) The construction of a fabric is a vital part of its design. Ability to design tends to grow with the acquisition of experience in and knowledge of the weaving craft. Weavers may design their own fabrics by beginning with stripes or plaids of different colors and of different size and textures of threads. See Figs. 45 and 46.

(3) The design of cloth is affected by the order in which the warp is put through the heddle eyes. When only two frames are used, the manner of threading is limited to the closeness or width in which the warp threads are spaced and the way they are grouped in the frames. Only a few threads may be grouped together, such as three or four, without weakening the fabric.

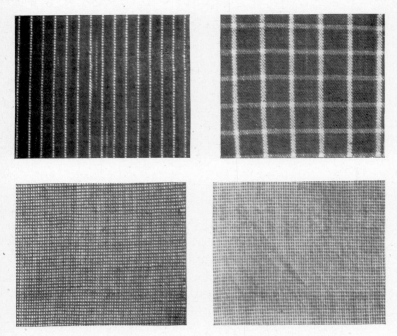

Fig. 45. Some fabrics woven on the kind of loom shown in Fig. 32.

They may be grouped evenly or unevenly — that is, one in the front frame and two in the back one. In most pattern weaving, more than two frames of heddles are used. As the number of frames increases, the variety of patterns that may be made increases.

Cloth on one set of warp may be woven with equal warp and weft showing, Fig. 8, No. 7, and Fig. 9, with no warp showing, Fig. 47, or no weft showing, Fig. 48. Cloth may be woven by taking the weft over groups of warp threads or by putting a number of weft threads side by side in one shed. Also, groups of warp threads may pass over groups of weft threads and the result is a basket weave. In Fig. 8, the pot holders numbered 4, 5, and 6, are woven in this way.

Fig. 46. Woven in stripes and plaids. *Loom Craft Studio, Wilmington, O.*

The spacing of warp depends on how it is threaded through the reed, such as one to a dent, two to a dent, or in unequal numbers such as one and then two in rhythmic order.

Patterns Are Called Drafts

There are patterns for threading, called threading drafts. They are helpful when more than two frames of heddles are used.

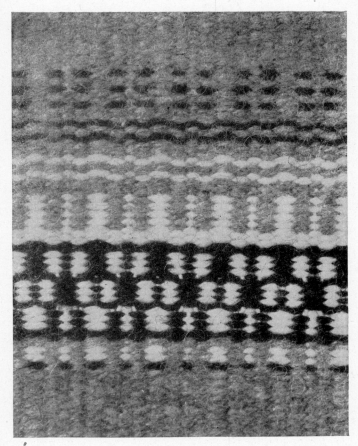

Fig. 47. Fabric woven with no warp showing. *Loom Craft Studio, Wilmington, Ohio.*

Though weaving with two frames of heddles is so varied that a weaver might specialize in it, most amateurs want to branch out into other fields and experiment with more and different ways of treadling. This involves not only learning to read threading, but also tie-up and treadling drafts.

Looms with several frames of heddles and the mechanism for moving them are frequently "tied-up" when they are pur-

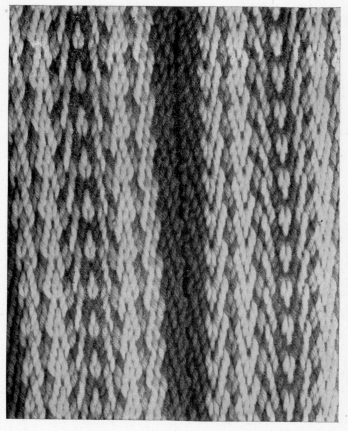

Fig. 48. Fabric with no weft showing. *Loom Craft Studio, Wilmington, Ohio.*

chased. The tie-up means the manner in which the treadles are attached to raise and lower the frames of heddles as wanted in making sheds. See Figs. 37 and 49.

Fourteen different sheds may be made on a loom having four frames of heddles, not counting those in which one shed above another is made simultaneously. The threads in each frame alone

72

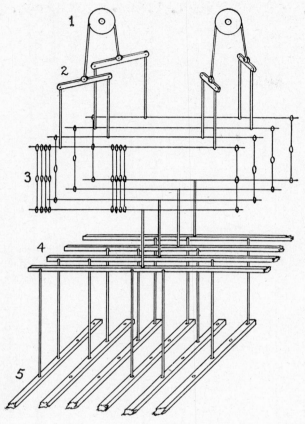

Fig. 49. Simplified diagram of complete harness of one type six-treadle, four-harness loom. This shows: 1, pulleys, 2, heddle horses, 3, heddle frames with heddles, 4, lams, and 5, treadles, and one way they may be tied together. Each treadle is tied to two lams and each lam to one frame.

may form the roof, Fig. 50, Nos. 2, 4, 6, and 8; or those in three of the frames may make the roof while those in the fourth make the floor, Fig. 50, Nos. 1, 3, 5, and 7. The two back frames may make the roof and the two front ones the floor, Fig. 51, No. 3, or this shed may be made in reverse, with the two front ones up

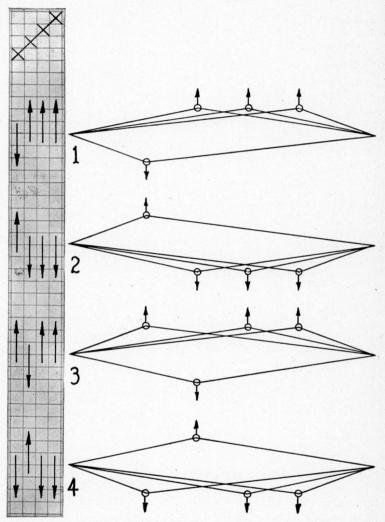

Fig. 50A. Diagrams in 50AB show the position of four frames, moving one against three, as the various treadles raise or lower them to make eight different sheds. The symbols used in drafts to indicate the frames are on the left at the top and the arrows point in the direction each frame is moved to make the shed at the right.

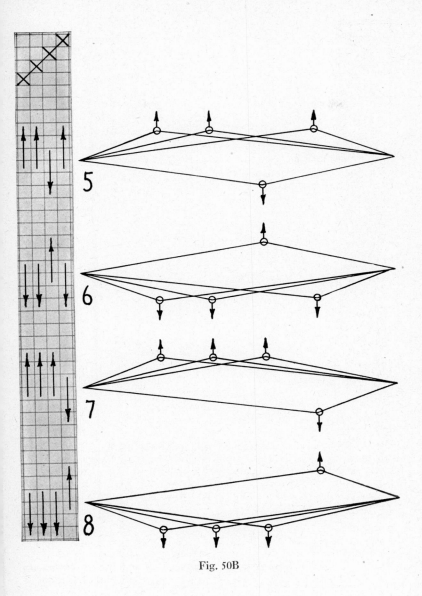

Fig. 50B

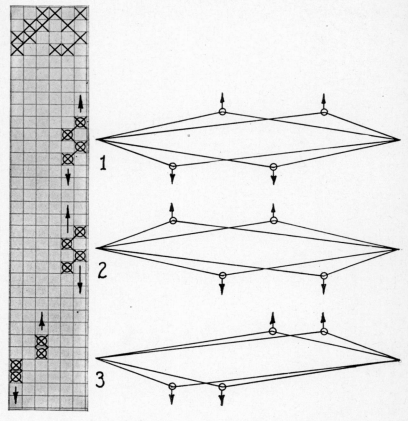

Fig. 51A. Diagrams in 51AB show the positions of four frames tied up to move two against two, as the six treadles moving them make six different sheds. The tie-up of the frames is indicated by the symbols on the left at the top. The arrows and symbols beside the diagram of each shed indicate which are raised and which are lowered.

and the two back ones down, Fig. 51, No. 4. The back and front ones may make the roof and the two middle ones the floor, Fig. 51, No. 5. This order may be reversed to make another shed, Fig. 51, No. 6. The back frame with the warp in the next-to-the-

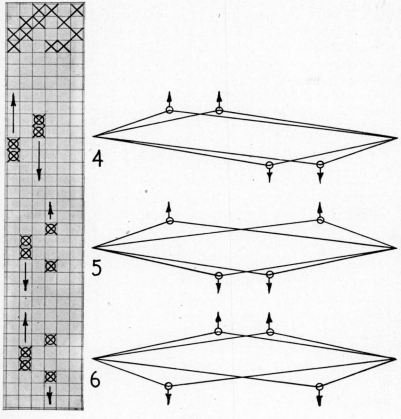

Fig. 51B

front frame may make the roof of another shed, while the front frame with its warp and the next-to-the-back may become the floor, Fig. 51, No. 1. These positions too may be reversed, Fig. 51, No. 2. The sum total of these sheds is fourteen different possibilities.

Some looms are tied up so that it is easy to make part of the sheds, such as one set of warp moving against three, Figs. 37

and 50, while others work better in raising a pair of frames at a time, Figs. 49 and 51. Looms may be tied up to make several combinations of sheds other than the above. See Fig. 52. The tie-up is changed to speed the weaving of certain patterns. More weaves can be made on looms tied up to move a single frame or frames in pairs than on those tied irregularly. The first type of loom tie-up requires four, the second six, and the third a variable number of treadles.

Selection of Treadles and Harnesses for a Loom

A six-treadle, four-harness loom is a good selection for the amateur, though he may choose one to which more harnesses and treadles may be added later.

Weaving Twills

The first thing to learn on a loom having more than two frames of heddles is to weave a twill. See Fig. 44. If the loom has an even number of frames of heddles, such as four, tabby also may be woven on it. When there are six treadles, two are for tabby, Fig. 51, Nos. 1 and 2, and the other four for twill and other pattern weaving. In Fig. 49, the two treadles at the extreme right are for tabby. Both twill and tabby may be used to form the binding or background for patterns requiring threadings which would leave weak places in the cloth.

A twill is threaded by beginning at the center or at either end of the front or the back frame. Weavers differ in their preferences, but most directions in books begin with the first heddle at the right in the back frame. However, beginning in the middle helps to center the weaving in the loom. A heddle in each frame is threaded in rotation until the number required is filled. A threading draft on squared paper, for a twill, looks like Fig. 52A. It is repeated as many times as is necessary to fill the reed with the closeness of warp and to the width desired. There is no difficulty in threading this pattern when beginning at the center.

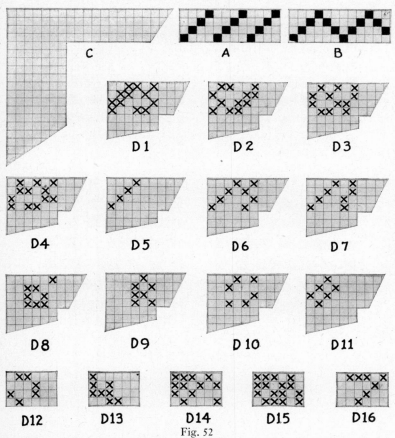

Fig. 52

Fig. 52. A — Draft showing the threading for a twill weave. B — Threading draft used in weaving which forms a diamond-like pattern. C — Outline for a weaving draft or pattern. The spaces between the horizontal lines across the page represent four frames of heddles. The six vertical spaces crossing them on the left, and extending downward, represent the six treadles. The 4 x 6, or 24, small squares in the rectangle made where the spaces cross represent both frames and treadles. This corner is used to show the tie-up of the treadles to the frames. D-1 — The draft of a common tie-up with two frames attached to each treadle. The tabby treadles are to the right. D-2-3-4 — Tabby treadles may be in any of these positions: at the left; in the center; center and left. They may be in reverse order or omitted but understood to be in the vacant spaces. D-7, D-15 — When the treadles in No. 7 go up, the treadles in No. 15 go down or vice versa. D-5-8-9-10-11-12-13-16 — The tie-up of other treadles may be omitted in the draft when they are not to be used for a pattern.

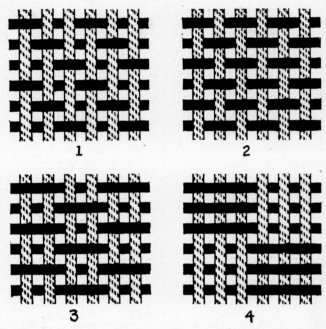

Fig. 53. Diagram of arrangement of warp and weft in cloth. No. 1 — Woven in twill (over one and under two). No. 2 — Tabby and plain weave (over one and under one). No. 3 — Basket weave (over two and under two). No. 4 — A variation of basket weave (under three and over three).

While tabby is formed by one weft thread crossing over and under alternate warp, Figs. 2 and 45, a twill is formed by going over one and under two, followed by the second weft going over the second warp and under the first and third. See Fig. 53, No. 1. The third weft follows by going under the first two and over the third. This order is repeated and gives a diagonal effect. It appears in the lowest white stripe in Fig. 44.

The least variation in threading a twill or in treadling produces a different result, as may be seen in Fig. 44. In many twills,

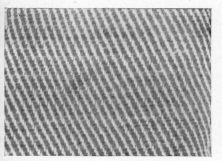

Fig. 54   Fig. 55

Fig. 54. Twill in which a white warp and a colored weft was used to make contrast. Fig. 55. The threading for this was done from back to front and then to back.

both sides of the fabric are the same. That is, both warp and weft are equally prominent, while in others either the warp or the weft may be more in evidence.

When treadling a plain twill on a loom with six treadles, the two reserved for tabby are not used. The other four treadles are pressed down one after another, making four sheds in rotation into each of which weft is shot. The same order of treadling is repeated until the piece of twill is completed. If the order of treadling is reversed, an arrowlike effect is produced. If the threading is changed so that it is put from back to front and then to back, Fig. 52B, a different pattern having an arrowlike shape results. Changes either in treadling, in threading, or in both will form diamonds and other patterns. See Figs. 54 and 55.

Tie-Up, Treadling, and Threading Drafts

A tie-up draft showing how the frames of heddles and treadles are attached to the rest of the harness is placed at one side of a pattern. See Fig. 52C. A common arrangement of a pattern is to have the horizontal lines, or rather the spaces between them extending across the paper from left to right, represent the frames

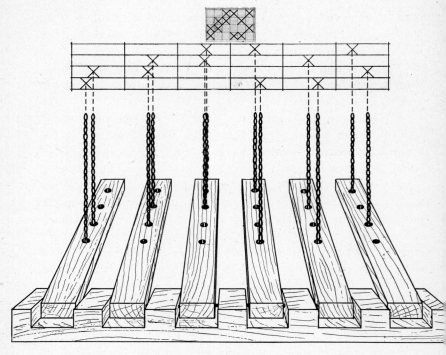

Fig. 56. A tie-up draft and a diagram showing the relation of treadles to the symbols and to the frames. Each frame in this tie-up is attached to or controlled by three different treadles, but only two frames are attached to each treadle. The near hole in each treadle is used for the near frame and the far hole for the far frame. When the tie-up is changed, the chains to the treadles are rearranged. In Fig. 52, D-8-9-13-14-15, the tie-up is changed so that three frames are attached to some treadles and only one to others.

of heddles. The six or more lines between the spaces at the left of the horizontal lines are extended downward to represent the treadles. For a four-heddle frame, six-treadle loom, this makes a diagram or draft with twenty-four little squares at the upper left-hand corner. The remaining space to the right between the horizontal lines is used for indicating the threading of the heddles in the frames. The spaces between the vertical lines are

82

used for the symbols which indicate the order of treadling. Fig. 56 shows the relation of heddle frames to the treadles and the symbols used in drafts for tie-ups.

Weavers using a draft can tell by looking at it what to do next as they weave, and it helps them to prepare the loom for making certain patterns.

To follow a draft made by someone else, one must know how the loom was tied up. Check the tie-up indicated at the upper left corner of the draft to see if it corresponds to the loom being used. See Fig. 52, D-1 to D-16. If the same, no difficulty will be found, but if different one may be able to use it by modifying the order of treadling. One must learn what drafts he can use and what ones will not fit his loom. The beginner had better select only those drafts adaptable to his loom. Patterns requiring eight heddle frames cannot be woven on a loom with but four, except by putting in much weft without the aid of heddles. This is not a practical way to weave. A draft shows what can be done on a loom. The tie-up of some looms is easily changed, while satisfactory adjustment is not attained in changing others.

A common tie-up for a loom with four frames of heddles and six treadles is to have each treadle attached to two frames. See Fig. 56. These may be attached directly to the frames. When a treadle is pressed down, the frames attached are pulled down, and the others balancing them are brought up, making a shed. This is a counterbalanced loom.

Lams

Some looms are equipped with lams. Lams are levers tied to the frames of heddles. The treadles are attached to the lams and manipulate them. Other looms have rollers which govern the action of the frame as the treadles are pressed. Directions from the manufacturer that are provided with a loom tell how it operates.

Tabby Treadles on a Four-Harness Loom

As mentioned before, tabby weave is used as a background, or in binding other weaves. It is commonly used at the beginning of a new piece of material and at its finish. This, for example, makes a better edge to hem, as tabby weaving is firm and not as thick as some other weaves. It may also be hemstitched.

A Variety of Common Tie-Ups

A common tie-up is for one treadle to raise the nearest and the farthest frame of heddles, Figs. 49 and 56. Another is the two nearest the weaver; another the two middle ones; and the remaining one the two farthest from the weaver. The two reserved for tabby are tied to alternating frames, that is, the back frame and the nearest center one to one treadle, and the front frame and the farthest center one to the other. In Figs. 49 and 56, they are at the right.

How Drafts Are Written

The makers of some drafts number while others letter the treadles and the frames. All do not do this in the same way, so drafts are very confusing to beginners. To avoid confusion, some authors omit all lettering or numbering and let the weaver learn the symbols for the frames of heddles and the treadles tied to them. One who learns to recognize the symbols has little difficulty in reading all drafts. Fig. 52D-1 to D-16.

Fig. 57. Symbols used in drafts to indicate treadling vary. In No. 1, the dashes indicate the order of treadling, beginning with the top line and reading down. In No. 2, the order of treadling is indicated by consecutive numbers. In the lower half, tabby is omitted. In the No. 3, the figure 2 indicates the number of times the treadle is pressed down. "Use tabby" is often written at the side of a treadling draft. It means that a tabby thread comes between each pattern thread. If written out in full, this draft would look like No. 4. No. 5 — Another order of treadling. No. 6 — The symbols indicate the kind or color of weft to put in when the shed is opened by the treadle in whose column its symbol is placed.

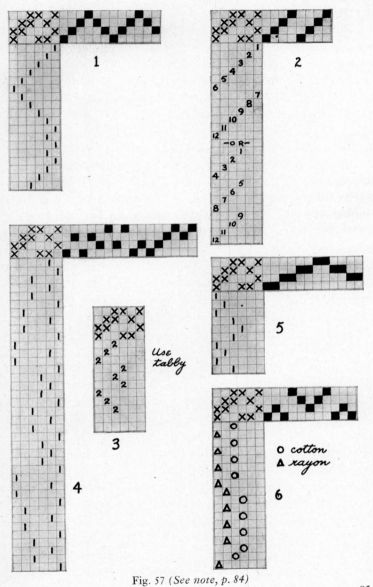

Fig. 57 (*See note, p. 84*)

(1) *Tie-up*. Learn to know which treadle on your loom is represented by each symbol. You can do this by following the trappings of the harness from the treadle to the frames of heddles it manipulates. See Figs. 49 and 56.

(2) *Treadling*. To read a draft, one notes where the symbols— that is, x's and o's — are located in the twenty-four little squares at the left corner, Fig. 52. One then reads the draft as one reads music. The first treadle to be pressed is indicated by a letter, number, or a dash in the top of the vertical space belonging to that treadle. See Fig. 57. The next one to be pressed is indicated under its proper treadle by a similar mark placed enough lower to indicate it is next. Read downward to follow treadling drafts. Sometimes after indicating tabby, the draft says "for 1 inch," "Use tabby," or "Tabby between," meaning that between each pattern thread there is a weft of tabby to make the cloth firmer or to form a part of the design. Then every tabby thread does not have to be indicated in the draft, but must not be forgotten. See Fig. 57, Nos. 3 and 4. In No. 3, the instructions read "Use tabby." No. 4 shows how this draft would look if written out in full. The weaver is expected to repeat the treadling until the fabric is complete.

Treadling Drafts or Instructions. Some records of treadling are made in the form of a table, in which case the treadles are each given a number. If that system is followed, it is a little more difficult to transpose the treadling of a pattern with a slightly different tie-up from that of the loom the weaver is using.

Some weavers try out different treadlings after their loom is tied-up and threaded, to find the one that works out best for the particular yarns they are using, and when they find one that suits they follow it for that particular piece of work. This is often a better method than trying to follow any given system of treadling.

(3) *Threading*. The threading is indicated by symbols in the horizontal spaces. Because there should be only one warp thread

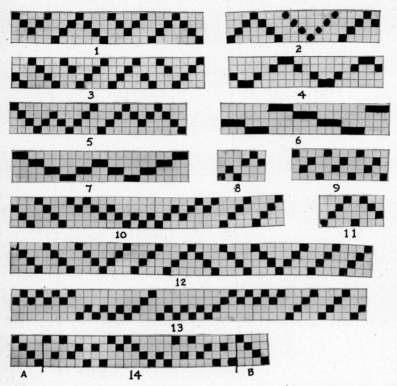

Fig. 58. Some common threading drafts for looms with four frames of heddles. The horizontal spaces between two lines represent a frame of heddles. The top one indicates the one farthest from the front of the loom, and the lowest one the nearest. Each small square in these spaces represents one heddle eye. A mark in a square indicates that one warp end or thread goes through the eye in this position. These drafts may be used with any of the tie-ups in Figs. 52D-1 and 57. The patterns shown are repeated all the way across in threading. Units of patterns may be combined to make others. Some units may be repeated oftener than others.

in each heddle, and the warp must all be parallel, no symbol in the threading draft comes directly over or below another. See Figs. 57, 58, and 59.

Symbols in Threading Drafts. Some symbols are used in

Fig. 59. Threading for looms making only two sheds.

threading drafts for grouping of warp threads in a dent, for one or more dents left empty, and for changes in color or texture of warp. The meaning of the symbols is written on the draft.

⌣ = All in one dent. Other symbols used may be ||, or |0| or |2|.

△ = One or more empty dents. Others used may be |ō| or *. Color symbols: red = X, blue = /, or green = O.

Texture: coarse = X, fine = /, rayon = O, or cotton =†.

As mentioned before, when tying up a loom, any pair of treadles may be for tabby. Therefore, on a draft they may be represented in any of the positions indicated in Figs. 52 and 57. By studying these drafts, a beginner should be able to recognize tabby combinations. The other four-treadle combinations may be recognized in the same way. They are arranged in three different pairs which are adjacent to one another, and a pair that has two spaces between. See Figs. 52D-1-2-3-4, 56, and 57.

Fig. 52D1-4 shows four different but complete tie-up drafts for the type loom we are describing. Six of the fourteen positions in which the frames may be in relation to each other may be attained with any one of these drafts. See Fig. 51. A pattern calling for one of them may be readily transposed to a loom with any of the other tie-ups. Many other looms are tied one treadle to one frame except for tabby treadles. See Fig. 52D-5-6-7.

Some Helpful Publications

Many articles and books have been published which contain weaving patterns. Among the more extensive ones is a book by

Marguerite P. Davidson, *Hand Weaver's Pattern Book*, 1944, published by the author, Strathmore, Pennsylvania. It contains drafts and pictures of many weaves of a great variety of types. Tie-up, threading, and treadling instructions are included in the drafts.

The Minister of Agriculture of Quebec, Canada, has several books on weaving for sale written both in English and in French, in which many beautiful fabrics are illustrated. The weaving drafts and suggestions for warp and weft accompany each illustration. They are by Oscar Beriau, and one of them, in French, is called *Tissage Domestique*. Another, in English, is *Home Weaving*, which is based on the first.

Two books by Lou Tate, a pamphlet based on the Little Loom House Country Fair and *Weaving Is Fun*, give suggestions for weaving on small looms of the table type having but two frames of heddles. They are published by the author, Kenwood Hill, Louisville 8, Kentucky.

Another is *Key to Weaving*, by Mary E. Black, published by Bruce, Milwaukee, which not only contains a great variety of weaving drafts with pictures of the fabrics developed from them but quite a comprehensive description of the construction of a large floor loom and directions for its operation. The weaves described are classified by the number of frames required on the loom, beginning with two and progressing up to eight or more, depending on the complexity of the work.

Check Treadles

When weaving for the first time on a new foot-power loom, check to see that the treadles are even when the frames are in neutral position, meaning neither up nor down and even with each other. If there are lams, they too must be parallel with one another, parallel with the heddle frames, and at right angles to the treadles. See Fig. 49. The foot or hand treadles should raise and lower the heddle frames easily and evenly. They should work smoothly and evenly enough so that a good weaver can put in one weft every three seconds.

Output of Weavers

A very rapid weaver has been known to make as much as fourteen yards in one day, rapid ones make about seven, but a beginner may make only a few inches. Fly-shuttle weaving is fast but noisy. For those who wish to produce fabrics for sale, it is useful; but for most of those who wish to weave for their own enjoyment, it is too strenuous. Our attention should be given to design, quality, and style, rather than quantity production.

Threading Patterns

Threading patterns are quite as numerous as dress patterns, and new ones appear frequently. Styles change in weaving; sometimes one type is popular and sometimes another. If the amateur knows a dozen or more main types of weaving patterns, he can obtain excellent results by modifying them to suit the yarns he has and the material he is making. See Figs. 57, 58, and 59.

Sizes of Yarns

Yarns are numbered in many ways by manufacturers. The Irish linens are numbered as 60/2, 40/3, 20/2, and so forth, down to 10/1. The first number indicates the size of the thread and the second number the twist or ply. The larger the size number the finer the thread used for making the twist. This makes a 10/1 the same size as a 20/2.

Cotton numbering varies considerably, some being numbered like linen, others marked by numbers alone or by notations. A number-20 cotton is customarily used for the warp and weft forming the tabby foundation of colonial types of weaving. For most cotton, the larger the number the finer the thread.

Wools are numbered in too many different ways and there are too many different kinds to specify numbers.

Steps in Weaving Patterns

Weaving patterns that require a tabby background may be done in the following order:

(1) Open the tabby shed.

(2) Throw the shuttle with the tabby weft through.

(3) Beat and check the tension of the thread.

(4) Following the draft, open the first pattern shed.

(5) Beat tabby with reed.

(6) Throw shuttle with pattern weft if different from the tabby and beat. If the same, use only one shuttle.

(7) Open other tabby shed.

(8) Beat.

(9) Put in tabby weft and repeat the weaving process in the order given above. Note there are two beats on each weft thread: one as soon as it is in the shed and one when the next shed is opened and before the following weft is put in. Use the same force and beat in pressing the weft into place throughout one piece of weaving to make it of even texture. When weaving, follow the predetermined order of treadling.

Temple

A temple or stretcher is a device used to help maintain the width of the material being woven. When using one, the weaver can give his attention to other phases of weaving and so work faster. See Fig. 13. On some small looms, the edges of the newly woven fabric may be tied to the sides of the loom frame to hold it full width. The ties have to be removed each time the cloth is rolled on the beam.

Slippage

When using rather smooth warp at a high tension, or when

raising or lowering the frames of heddles changes the tension of the warp, some weaves have a tendency to slip at the point of passing over the cloth beam, making the cloth look as if it had been carelessly woven. See Fig. 23. This may be overcome by different methods, depending on the fabric being made.

(1) Avoid having the warp tighter than need be to make a cloth of the desired firmness — that is, closeness of weft thread.

(2) A smooth paper laid over the breast beam will permit the cloth to move a bit without slipping the weft out of place.

(3) A roller attached to the front of the breast beam prevents slippage in delicate fabrics.

(4) For very loose and soft fabrics, the roller may be wrapped with sandpaper.

(5) The cloth beam may be wrapped with a blanket to make it give a little.

Some slippage may be taken out by stretching the finished fabric on the bias and then on the straight until the weft is worked back into place. Gentle brushing may help; but it is best to avoid slippage in the first place.

Selvage in Pattern Weaving

No matter what pattern is being followed, the selvage, made of six or eight warp at each side, should always be threaded so that alternate ends of warp are raised and lowered for each pick. They are often threaded two or more to a dent. This is done to make the material as firm as possible. Some pattern drafts show selvage threading and some do not. Generally a twill will make the desired selvage, but sometimes the threading must be carefully worked out to obtain a proper edge.

Records of Work

Records of work should be kept so that the weaver may not forget what he has done. The records should include sizes, brand, and kind of yarn used as well as drafts followed.

RECORD CARD

Woven by_____ Date_____

Name of weave_____

Kind and size or number of warp_____

Kind or kinds and size or number of weft_____

_____

No. of reed_____ Warp to a dent_____

No. of warp threads_____ No. of inches wide in reed_____

Width of finished material_____

Tie-up   Threading draft

Treadling draft

(Notes and special instructions)

Dressing for Warp

A flaxseed dressing may be used on wool as well as linen warp to facilitate weaving. Soak the seed several hours, then boil until the liquid is thick like coffee cream. Strain. Wet the warp, dip into the seed solution, and hang up to dry. This solution soon spoils, so only the amount needed at the time should be made. Wet wool warp is stronger than dry.

Finishes for Weaving

When the weaving is finished and the article hemmed or a fringe knotted in the ends, it should be pressed lightly under a damp cloth. Pressing too hard may destroy the texture of the weaving.

How to Convert a Table or Hand-Power Loom Into a Foot-Power Loom

The advantage of foot power over hand power is that it frees both hands for other operations. Holes are made in the top of the table on which the loom is to stand, so it must be sturdy. Fig. 31. Treadles are mounted on a board with blocks of wood nailed to it between which the treadle sticks are placed. A horizontal hole is bored through the treadle ends and through the blocks. A bolt or metal rod is driven through the holes to act as a hinge for the treadles. The opposite ends of the treadles are attached to the frames of the loom by a cord or a chain. Each cord passes through the table top directly under the frame of heddles to which it is to be attached. This makes one hole almost back of the other. See Figs. 49 and 56.

Profits of Weaving

Weaving is a pleasurable pastime and it may be turned into a profitable one, for there is a ready market for good products with style. It is important to aim at producing not only well-made but interesting fabrics with a flair about them. Otherwise, one may as well buy ready-made materials.

Variety of Weaves in This Chapter

The weaver should now know how to weave twill and the many variations that may be woven with the twill threading by changing the order of treadling; to weave tabby or plain weave on a four frame loom; and to make a greater variety of useful articles in more interesting weaves too numerous to name. Fig. 23 shows the arrangement of warp and weft in cloth woven in twill, tabby, or plain weave, and two basket weaves.

CHAPTER V

Pattern Problems

Patterns for weaving can be divided into sections or units. Many of these units may be combined to make more varied designs. Some of the common threading units are those which make tabby, twill, and stripes. Fig. 59 shows some two-frame pattern units. The most common four-frame pattern units are as illustrated in Figs. 57 and 58.

Right and Wrong Sides of Fabrics

Reversible fabrics have no right and wrong side. Some fabrics simply have a design on one side that is different from that on the other. See Fig. 60. Either may be used as the "right" side. The contrast in the colors chosen and the textures of the warp and weft will help determine which side should be the "right." Others have right and wrong sides; in these the design is on the right side, while the other shows the warp and weft threads which are not needed in the pattern but must be carried to another place. See Fig. 43C. Sometimes weft ends show on the wrong side. When the warp is unattractive and entirely covered on the right side of the material, as in brocades, the cloth has a definite wrong side.

Names of Threading Patterns

Some types of threading patterns have been given names, and several designs have been called by the same name. Tabby

Fig. 60. By reversing the treadling following the plain tabby in the center, this illustration shows how both sides of the fabric looks. Either may be used as the right side. *Woven in Loom Craft Studio, Wilmington, Ohio.*

is the plain weave on a two-harness loom or the same weave made on those with more harnesses. Stripes, plaids, and basket weave are well known. This last, however, is applied to patterns which seem wholly unrelated. Other well-known names are twill, rose path, m's and o's, honeysuckle, herringbone, diamond, summer and winter, birdseye, huck and check. There are several ways of threading called rose path. This is true of other threadings.

Producing Different Effects on One Threading

When the loom is threaded according to a given draft, different effects may be produced. Fig. 61 shows a variety of designs in one piece of fabric. The warp was threaded using a rose-path draft like Fig. 58, No. 1. The kind and color of weft was changed from stripe to stripe in the first half of the piece and repeated in most of those in the second half. A bonding weft like the warp was also used in some and not in others. The treadling pattern was changed in many places. Some of the designs are the reverse of others like Nos. 1 and 2 in Fig. 60. That is, when the cloth is turned over, 1 looks like 2 and 2 like 1. Some of the weft was smooth and some was knobby. A whole piece of cloth might be woven like any one of these numerous stripes. See Fig. 61.

Twill, Figs. 52A and 57, No. 2, is another threading from which a variety of effects may be produced. Also see Figs. 23 and 44. Many of these are arrowlike or in broken twills and others are zigzags. By using the same treadle several times, a very different effect may be produced by this threading, as seen in the center of Fig. 23.

Limitations in Pattern Weaving

The patterns that may be developed on a loom when making no shed may be of any size and as complicated, varied, and exotic as the weaver may choose, for any color or texture may be put in at any point desired.

When the loom provides for making two sheds, the weaving patterns become simpler. One or more shuttles may be used to help vary the pattern, but in all instances a row of weft has to go across the web and be beaten down so that the next row

98

Fig. 61. A variety of weaving designs in one piece of fabric. The threading for this material was Fig. 58, No. 1. The kind and color of weft used
was changed from stripe to stripe, and the treadling was different in different stripes. In some a binding weft was used and not in others. Some
of the designs were the reverse of the others. In this sample, much of the
lower half was woven in reverse of the upper.

will be parallel with it. The pattern in two-shed weaving may be varied by using the processes of weaving without a shed, but in combination with it. Of course, this slows the process but may be well worth the time. See inlays in Fig. 26. The edge of the sample in Fig. 26, No. 2, has Ghiordes knots between the picks of plain weaving at the lower edge. Such an edge is effective on drapes and if put on all sides for pillow tops. For these tops there should be an edge of plain weaving of at least half an inch for use in sewing the pillow cover together. Ghiordes and other knots may be used to develop stripes in draperies and to give them an interesting texture.

Looms having four frames of heddles are capable of making a greater variety of patterns — that is, arrangements of the warp and weft threads—because of the fact that fourteen sheds may be made on them. However, as has been pointed out, only about half this number of sheds is made on any one loom for a given piece of work. Beside this, the number of frames controls one feature of the pattern, for one frame cannot be left idle for many picks, else there would be weak places in the cloth. In other words, though the patterns made on a four-frame loom are composed of a great variety of differences, the motifs in them are smaller than those seen in many manufactured fabrics which may be woven on looms of more complicated models. The designs resulting from a four-frame loom are quite conventional-ized and repeated often, except when handwork is inserted in them, or changes in texture and color of weft give them variety. Floral designs cannot be woven on them, though the names of some patterns are for flowers such as wild rose and honeysuckle. These are so conventionalized that it takes a stretch of the imagination to see the slightest resemblance to the flowers.

Weavers Often Specialize

Weaving patterns dependent on the threading of the warp require much patient threading of the heddles if the designs are

100

changed often, so some weavers prefer to use but one type or draft for threading and vary their patterns by the combinations of treadling and the kinds, colors, and methods of inserting the weft. As the warp is used up, these weavers merely tie new warp to the ends of the old and do not need to worry about the threading. Some of the most common threadings used on four-harness looms to get texture results are twill, honeysuckle, rose path, and m's and o's.

How Textures May Be Developed in Fabrics

(1) *Laid-in Designs.* Weavers sometimes put a length of yarn into the shed with the weft to make an initial letter or other motif in the weaving. This may be turned back and forth at the points desired as is done in tapestry weaving. Fig. 26, Nos. 1 and 2. Short lengths of bright yarn laid in at regular intervals add interest to a rug or fabric which otherwise might be quite dull.

(2) *Overshot Weaves.* A four-harness loom is required for overshot weaves, except for the very small pieces which can be made on a picture frame. A shuttle for fine binding weft and another for coarse filling complete the equipment. The filling or pattern threads are packed or beaten closely to cover the warp. The sequence of using the shuttles should be followed carefully. The binding tabby should be in 50/50 weave. The correct ratio between tabby and pattern weft must be found by making a test sample. See Fig. 62.

(3) *Weaves Requiring Multiple Weft in Each Shed.* Weaves requiring two or three weft threads in each shed without tabby between look better if the weft is put in with as many shuttles as there are to be threads in a shed. One is put in and beaten into place and the next one put in from the opposite side and beaten. If there is a third, it follows from the first side. Then the new shed is opened and the above steps repeated when a number of weft together are needed.

Fig. 62. Overshot weave. (Weft is sidewise in this picture.) The warp and the weft used for tabby are linen. The wool weft alternating with the linen goes over six warp and then under and over seven, which is repeated. Halfway up, the wool goes under one warp after skipping over six, then goes over five and under one. This too is repeated for several picks. The overshot wool weft is cut at the right to form a pile.

(4) *Seersucker and Other Puckered Goods.* One stripe of nonelastic warp and the next one of elastic preshrunk will, after laundering, result in a material with puckered stripes.

(5) *Picking up the Weft.* Textures may be developed by drawing up loops in the weft. This is done by putting in a loose weft and picking it up between given numbers of warp, and holding loops in place with a knitting needle or some other article until the background weaving has progressed enough to fix them. See Fig. 63.

(6) *Using a Second Warp Beam.* To weave warp loops in a fabric, a second warp beam is required. This may be attached to the loom or hang free with enough weight to give the warp

102

Fig. 63. Pick-up weave in which a loose weft of rayon is picked up between the linen warp at regular intervals and held in place with a knitting
needle until the background tabby weaving with linen weft will hold
them in place.

proper tension. The warp on the second beam may be threaded
into every fourth dent and is generally heavier than the foundation yarn. The weaving proceeds as usual until loops are wanted
from the second beam. These warp threads are then raised and a

103

Fig. 64. Loops woven with a second warp beam. A linen background, with rayon and wool warp from a second warp beam, was woven in with the linen tabby. When loops were desired, the warp on the second beam, which was all threaded through the heddles in one frame, was raised and a dowel rod put through the shed to pull this warp forward. The tabby weaving then proceeded to hold it in place, and the rod was removed to use in making the next loops.

rod put in the shed to pull them forward the amount desired. While being held in this position, the loops are firmly fastened in the web by at least three shots of regular weaving. See Fig. 64.

Fig. 65. Three doll-house rugs being woven simultaneously. Note dowel rod, as in Fig. 21.

Narrow Fabrics Woven Side By Side

Gimp is often needed to match home-woven upholstery material. As it is usually ½ to 2 inches wide, it may be woven simultaneously in two or more webs. Ten or more warp threads and at least one shuttle for each strip are required for narrow gimp. The weaving of each strip is done by turns and progresses evenly if the beater is used. If a comb is used as a beater, one strip may be completed and then another up to the point where the warp must be unrolled. Larger articles may be woven in pairs. See Fig. 65 and the napkins in Fig. 42.

Buttonholes

Buttonholes are woven by using the same method as for two strips of fabric for part of the way; that is, the cloth is woven clear across. Then, using two shuttles, turn each back where the buttonhole is to be formed. When the open space in the fabric is completed, the weaving continues clear across the web until time to make the next buttonhole.

Fringe

Fringe is woven like gimp except that two rows of fabric are woven at a time, with a space between them across which the weft passes. There may be several pairs on the loom. The headings of a pair should be spaced ½ to 5 or 6 inches apart.

Occasionally, a few weft are turned back between the groups of weft passing from one web to the other at the edge from which the fringe extends, to keep this edge of the web from raveling. When the weaving is completed, the fringe is cut apart between the two headings.

Leno or Lace Weaves

Leno means a thin, open cloth. Leno and lace weaves are often formed by leaving unthreaded dents in the reed while putting groups in other dents. See Figs. 66 and 67. Warp threaded in groups, leaving open dents between, woven without beating the weft too closely, is the simplest method of making leno cloth. Open weaves also are made by picking up some warp and twisting it over or under adjoining threads as in the border of Fig. 68 and the ends of Figs. 66 and 70; or by bringing the shuttle around groups of warp and drawing them together with the weft. See Fig. 69. Another decorative weave is sometimes called Spanish lace weave. See Fig. 70. After some plain weaving is completed, the shuttle is put through the next shed to the point where an eyelet is to be made, then returned to the selvage in another shed and back again in the next shed, where it crosses the eyelet and goes on to the next one to be formed. From there it is returned to the warp at the side of the first eyelet and back again. The shed is changed each time the

Fig. 66. The same Bronson lace weave as in Fig. 67, used as a border around a square. (Warp is sidewise in this display.) On the end are two rows of pick-up weaving in which the warp is twisted in two ways. In the top row, two warp from the upper shed were twisted over two in the lower shed; in the bottom row, two adjacent warp were twisted over the next two, and the weft put through to hold them in place.

weft is put in. This procedure is continued all across the web and the shuttle returned in the same manner to the side where the weaving was begun. Most of these require much handwork, so are slow processes. They are suitable for making borders and special motifs in other weaves.

Double-Surface Weaving

Double-surface weaving results in two fabrics one over the other. The pattern is produced by crossing the two webs along the lines of the figures in the pattern. Two colors, such as blue and white, were used in old coverlets of this weave. A cloth

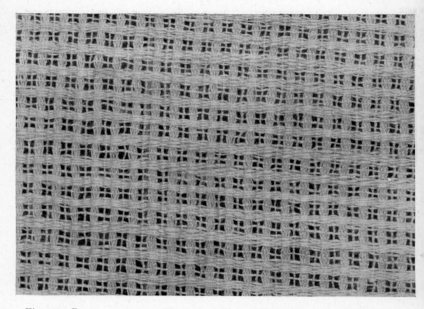

Fig. 67. Bronson-pattern ("barleycorn" threading) lace weave. The warp was grouped in some of the dents of the reed while other dents were skipped. The weft also was beaten closely and then lightly to leave spaces between. *Loom Craft Studio, Wilmington, Ohio.*

known as "summer and winter" because it has a dark and a light side is one of the varieties of double-surface weaving. In it, the pattern is interwoven with the ground more often than usual.

Double Weaving

When double-surface weaving is made so there is no thread crossing from the top fabric to the under one, there are two pieces of cloth. See Fig. 71. There is no advantage in making two separate fabrics in this way; but if one wants a woven piece of tubing, it may be made by using one shuttle and carrying it from the upper to the lower web at each pick, thus making a complete circle with the shuttle through the two webs.

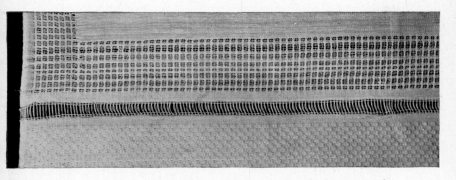

Fig. 68. A border made in pick-up lace weave in which groups of warp threads are twisted over and under adjoining threads while others were put in like Bronson and tabby weaves.

Fig. 69. Another type of pick-up lace weave in a wide border in which the weft is put around groups of warp drawing them together to form an openwork pattern.

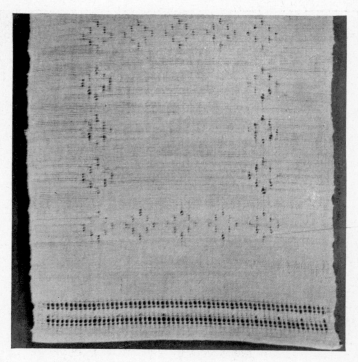

Fig. 70. A weave sometimes called Spanish lace. The warp is pulled apart where the weft is turned back, thus making little slits in the cloth. The slits form the pattern. See diagram 1, Fig. 14. The border on the end is a pick-up weave like the upper one in Fig. 66, except that when the first row and several picks of tabby were in place, a weft thread was used to draw the tabby together after each fifth group of twisted warp, and then the second row of pick-up was made.

If a piece of coarse material is wanted wider than the loom reed, it may be made by carrying the shuttle in double weaving around and back to close one selvage and leave the other open. Such material may be twice the width of the reed. A plain twill draft is followed for making this material.

Double face and double weaving can be made most easily on four-frame looms that are not counterbalanced, as on these

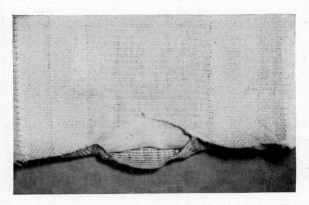

Fig. 71. Double weaving in which a pocket is left showing the two layers of cloth woven one above the other. The remainder of the double weaving was occasionally caught together by bringing warp from the lower part to the top. This weave makes cloth with the two sides in different colors. It is a weave better suited to a loom with eight or more frames of heddles.

one warp at a time is brought to the top and three to the bottom of the web. When the frames are balanced two against two, the warp in the two back frames of heddles may make the top and that in the two front ones the bottom fabric. When twill threading is used, each fabric is in tabby. Double face and double weaving are better suited to looms having eight or more frames of heddles.

Bead Weaving

One method of bead weaving requires a warp without a shed. A strong warp suited to the size of the beads is threaded into the loom and spaced so that the beads will fit closely between the strands. A strong weft is threaded into a long, fine needle, while the beads are strung on a similar weft. The beads on the string are pushed up between the warp and the needle is put through them above the warp thus locking them in place. The beads have to be strung in proper order to make a pattern. For a narrow band they may consist of two black beads, a red one, a white one, a blue one; then a white one, a red one, and lastly two black ones. There must be one more warp thread than there are beads in the pattern. In the above example, there would be ten warp threads, as nine beads are to be in a row.

Another method is to have the needle threaded, take up a bead, and put the thread through it above the warp. When the row is completed put in another weft from underneath the warp, going through each bead.

A third way is to string the beads on the warp and weave tabby between them.

Card Weaving

Card weaving, sometimes called tablet weaving, is a form in which the warp threads are put through holes in the corners of heavy cards two to three inches square. The cards take the place of heddles in their frames and the holes the heddle eyes. This kind of weaving is used to make narrow, thick, strong articles like belts.

There are different ways of holding the warp to keep it in order and of proper tension. A sensible way is to use warp wound on a board loom. See Fig. 7. The warp ends are attached to the pairs of sticks which may serve as warp and cloth beams. This is done after the cards have been threaded.

The cards may have square corners but are better if they are slightly rounded. The holes may be punched with a paper punch. Marking the front and back of each and lettering or numbering the holes helps to keep the cards in order and to put one back if it gets out. An even number of cards seems to work better.

In learning to weave, do not worry about a pattern. Choose the colors of warp wanted, such as red and white, or white, gray, and red. Decide which color is to be at the outside edges and thread all the holes of the first and last cards with this color. The other threads may be hit and miss, or arranged in corresponding pairs in the cards, or the cards arranged in corresponding pairs as are the outside two. The threads may be put through all the holes from front to back, all from back to front, or half from front to back and the other half in reverse. If this last threading is used, care must be taken to thread and keep the cards in corresponding pairs. That is, the third card from each end would constitute a pair and should be threaded with the same colors of warp in corresponding holes. If the cards are kept in order while weaving, this will make the pattern which develops alike on each side of the center.

First, learn to handle the cards with dexterity. The weft may be in a shuttle of the flat or the pick-up type. Rubber bands are handy to keep the cards in order if they are to be left for a time.

Start weaving with a rather tight warp. Holding the cards in order, remove the band, and turn them so that all the corners marked B, for instance, replace those marked A. Replace the band and put the weft in the shed in the warp. Turn the cards to C and again put in weft. After a little experience the elastic band is not needed. If the warp has not become too tight, turn the cards so that the corner D is where A was originally. Several turns may be made in this direction. In time, the warp will become quite tight. The next step is to turn the cards in reverse back to C, then to B, and finally to A, putting in the weft at each turn. The weaver may continue turning in the reverse order until the warp becomes tight, when he changes the direction of the turns and weaves until it is tight again. He will soon see that making the same number of turns, such as seven, in each direction, develops a definite pattern. He will also note that at the points where he changes the direction of the turning of the cards a long stitch results, but as this comes at regular intervals it forms a part of the pattern.

A record should be kept of the threading, the arrangement of the cards, and the number of turns made in each direction, in order to duplicate a pattern, or to continue if one has to leave

113

Fig. 72. Two types of inkle looms and a reel for unwinding skeins of yarn.
Loom Craft Studio, Wilmington, Ohio.

the weaving for a time. To rip out weaving, reverse the turns and take out the weft. As a weaver becomes expert, groups of the cards may be turned in different directions to develop other patterns, and the threading may follow a preconceived plan or pattern. Care must be taken in putting in the weft either to avoid loops at the edges or to make even loops all along. Weft must be at uniform tension to make a neat band.

Weaving on an Inkle Loom

The inkle loom is an arrangement of pegs around which warp is wound so that the warp may be pushed along after the weft is put in. This makes belts and other narrow bands in a warp face weave which has somewhat the appearance of card weaving. See Fig. 72. A shuttle and a flat stick for putting in and beating

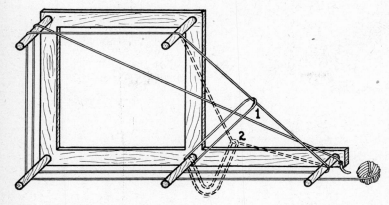

Fig. 73. Diagram showing how an inkle loom is warped and where the two sheds are formed.

down the weft are needed. The warp is fastened at peg B. Two sheds are made. See Fig. 73.

Variety of Weaves in This Chapter

This chapter has treated of: (1) Weaving two or more fabrics side by side, as can be done when making gimp, fringe, and buttonholes. (2) Threading patterns and the numerous ways in which they may be treadled. (3) Reversible fabrics. (4) Surface patterns like brocades. (5) Overshot weaves which when cut results in chenilles. (6) Laid-in designs. (7) Basket and other multiple-weft fabrics. (8) Seersucker. (9)Pick-up, in which weft loops form a pattern. (10) The use of a second warp beam in making loops of warp. (11) The leno weaves, many of which are called lace weaves, such as pick-up, Spanish, Bronson, and lace. (12) Double face weave and double weaving. A form of this latter is called summer and winter. (13) Bead weaving. (14) Card weaving. (15) Weaving bands on an inkle loom.

INDEX

117

118